STILL LIFE DRAWING

PETER STANYER &
TERRY ROSENBERG

ARCTURUS

INTRODUCTION

There are many ways in which we can understand and express our ideas, observations and feelings through drawing, and it is important that you embark on this drawing course without any preconceptions. Many students, particularly beginners, start out with very narrow opinions about art and drawing, adopting a fixed attitude as to what a drawing should be and how it should appear. In particular, they think that a drawing should be an exact copy of the reality it is taken from. Yet this is an impossible task, and when students try to achieve this idea of copying reality, they ultimately fail.

When you stand in front of a still-life subject and try to draw, you can easily become overwhelmed by the subject because you do not know how to approach it. But if you take the attitude of breaking down and simplifying the subject in front of you, this makes the process of drawing more manageable and accessible, particularly if you are a beginner. As an example, in one of the projects that follow you will approach the still life by looking at its textures and finding ways to create the illusion of texture through drawing. In another project you will observe light and shadows on the still life, and concentrate on describing just this aspect of the subject.

The different ways of looking at and understanding what you see are as important as the physical act of making a drawing. Each of the following chapters presents a particular way of looking at still life – through light, shape, texture, form, space and movement – and then introduces techniques that you can use to describe that way of looking. It is important that you start with Chapter 1 and work through the subsequent chapters in sequence, as projects later in the book often

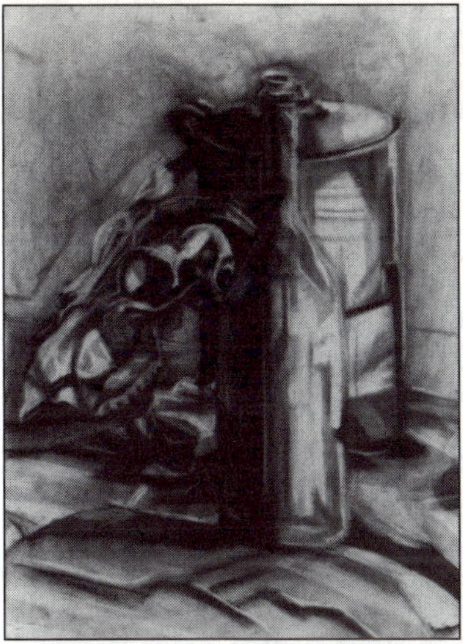

Still life seen as form, light and space

refer back to earlier projects and chapters.

Until relatively recently, still life was cast aside by theorists and was not recognised as a subject of any real importance. Yet, since the times of ancient Greece artists have used still life in many forms as a means of recording everyday life. It is the stuff that reflects our historical and cultural activity and the evidence of our domestic lives. Insignificant objects can be given significance and any object can be given symbolic meaning. The consistent attention and fascination of artists towards still life has proved its worth and brought it critical attention and approval, elevating it to its rightful place in the history of art. In each chapter, the art historical context is given for the approach to drawing that is being tackled, and specific works and artists are suggested for study that will help you with your own drawing.

By the end of the book you should have gained a broad experience of ways of drawing that will enable you to use a number of procedures to express your ideas and observations. You may find that you enjoy and respond to some projects very positively, whereas you will find other projects difficult to get to grips with, but this is all part of finding out where your strengths and interests lie.

CHAPTER 1

SPACE AND LIGHT

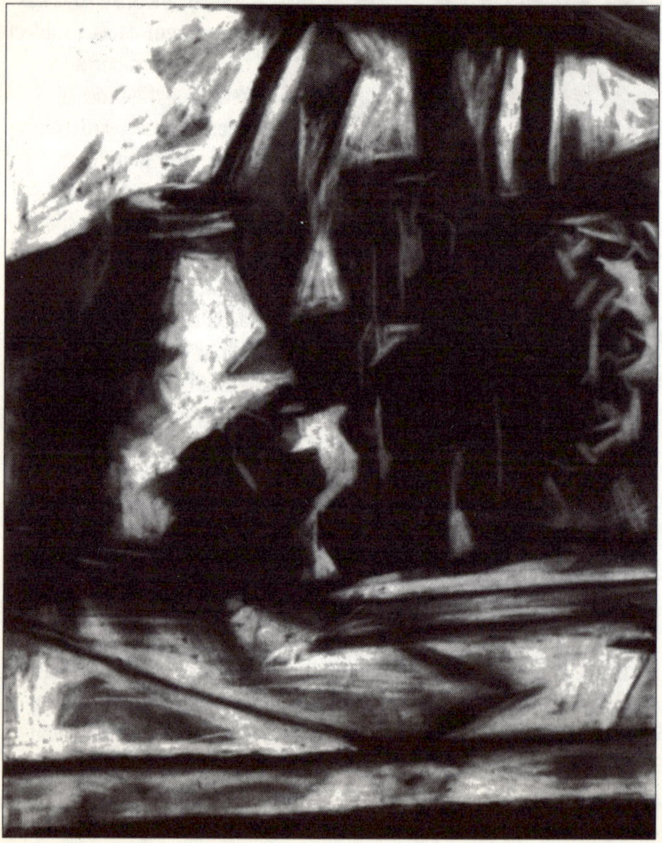

When we look at the world, we often take what we see for granted. The purpose of this chapter is to encourage you to re-understand your everyday visual experiences and interpret them afresh by introducing a way of seeing based on ideas about space and tone. At the end of the projects, you should be able to construct a drawing, as many artists have done before, using the techniques of negative space and chiaroscuro (extremes of light and dark) and the basics of proportion.

The drawings are all based on observation: what we see, and how we understand, formulate and interpret this. However, when you are making a drawing bear in mind that you are not trying to reproduce 'the truth' of what you see. Your aim should be to make an interpretation or expression from your observations and knowledge of the subject. You cannot possibly include everything about the subject in a drawing; you have to be selective and discerning by taking a particular approach each time. And by gaining a basic but broad experience of different approaches, you will be able to develop your own work further.

NEGATIVE SPACE

Negative space is the space around objects. It links the objects together and helps us to see the composition as a whole. As such, it is the underlying structure that forms the composition. We usually look at and recognise objects, but are seldom aware of the spaces between them. However, if you draw objects as individual items without considering the spaces between them, they tend to have no relationship to one another and will float in a void.

If you draw using negative space, this places the objects in a context and sets up relationships between them. An example of a work in which the use of negative space is important is *The Battle of San Romano* by Paolo Uccello (1396/97-1475), in which the shapes between the horses' legs, for example, are as considered as the actual legs themselves. This use of negative space helps to guide the eye through the composition. Edgar Degas (1834-1917) was also a master of negative composition, especially in his paintings and drawings of race horses. Also worth looking at is Vincent van Gogh's (1853-90) *Sunflowers*; notice the shapes he has created between the flowers.

CHIAROSCURO

By using a strong light to illuminate a still-life arrangement, you can create very dark shadows and bright, light areas. You can then add tone to the drawing to express this extreme example of light and dark, which is known as chiaroscuro. There are many good examples of artists who have used chiaroscuro in their work, but possibly the artist who is most closely associated with the technique is Carravaggio (1571-1610). He used tone in an organised, formal way (for modelling forms, or differentiating between objects or planes in space), in contrast to Rembrandt (1606-69), who used the extremes of light and dark to create a dramatic, atmospheric effect. This latter approach to tone is the method that you will use in this chapter. The more formal aspects of tone are covered in later chapters.

MEASUREMENT AND PROPORTION

The positions and proportions of the objects in your set-up remain constant throughout the drawing, and this enables you to judge whether you have drawn them accurately (except, of course, when you want to distort the shape, form or size of objects deliberately). Although measuring is important for most drawings, do not worry about being absolutely accurate. Be as accurate as necessary for the drawing. The still-life arrangement is the starting point for your drawing, a reference to help you, but you are not reproducing it exactly. From time to time, ask yourself whether the proportions of the objects look right. If not, correct them using the still-life arrangement to help you.

PROJECT 1

NEGATIVE SPACE AND CHIAROSCURO

One 6-hour drawing (including setting up)

Materials: *still-life objects, white sheet or paper for background, spotlight or anglepoise lamp, window-mount, A1 cartridge paper, charcoal, compressed charcoal, eraser*

Selecting still-life objects

Your choice of objects is important. It is very easy to select things that are not appropriate for this exercise, while by choosing the right objects you can avoid all kinds of unnecessary problems and side issues. Do not use objects that have any decoration on them, because at this point patterns and decoration will create confusion. Also, do not choose any transparent objects such as bottles or glasses. Wine bottles that have been painted with white or black emulsion paint to make them opaque are very good.

You will need about half a dozen objects with simple forms: for example, a vase, a house brick, a jug, a casserole dish, a painted bottle, a stoneware mustard-pot and so on. Make sure that the objects are different sizes, forms and tones. For instance, you could choose a small, dark, rectangular object, a tall, thin, white, cylindrical object, and a fat, squat, spherical object. So even before you start to draw, your subject matter will consist of an array of simple objects that already possess different characteristics.

Creating the setting

Push a table flush against a wall and cover it with white paper or a white sheet. If the wall is not white or a plain, light colour, cover the area directly above and behind the table with white paper or a white sheet as well. It is necessary to push the table up against the wall for two reasons. First, this limits the depth of field, or the distance from the front to the back of the area you are drawing, and eliminates any unnecessary objects from the background that might appear if the table was in the middle of the room. Second, and more importantly, an artificial horizon line is created where the top of the table meets the wall. This line is crucial because it is your starting point for the negative-space drawing, and you will be assessing the objects in the picture plane against it.

Arranging the still life

Having collected together your objects, you need to consider how to arrange them for the drawing. Ad hoc arrangements sometimes work perfectly well, but for this exercise it is best to think about your arrangement before you proceed. Most importantly, avoid a symmetrical arrangement – one with the tall objects at each end and the rest gradually diminishing in size towards the centre. Another unsuitable arrangement would be with all the tall objects at one end, gradually diminishing down to the smallest objects at the other end. Neither do you want to place the objects in a straight line across the table. You need to make a small but interesting depth of field by overlapping some objects one in front of another. Nor should each object stand in isolation; one or two standing on their own is all right, but not all six. Finally, the dark objects should not be grouped together at one end of the composition and the light objects at the other.

The first time that you attempt this project, place yourself directly in front of the group if possible. Try out a number of different arrangements until you are satisfied with one that appears to be balanced and rhythmical without being too ordered. Once the group is set up, make a small, quick, outline drawing from your proposed drawing position. Look at your sketch and decide if the composition works; if not, make any adjustments that you feel would improve it.

Using a window-mount

To select your composition, hold up the window-mount towards the still-life group and look through it. If you are right-handed, use your left hand to hold the mount, and vice versa if you are left-handed. Always try to look

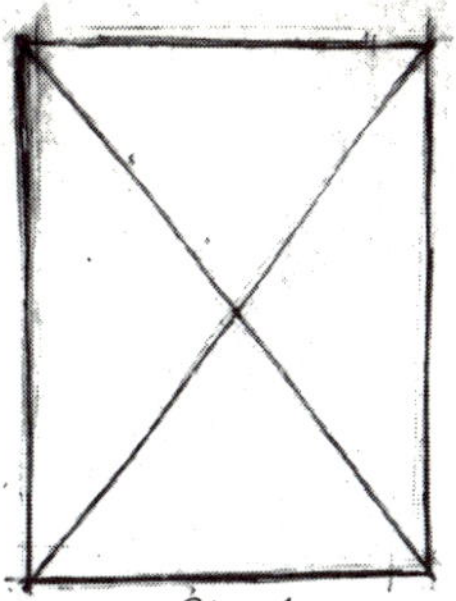

Step 1

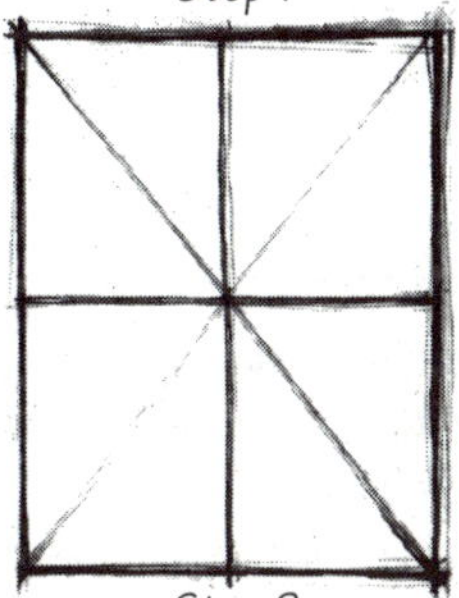

Step 2

HOW TO MAKE A WINDOW-MOUNT

A window-mount is a very useful device for framing and organising a composition. You can buy plastic mounts with a grid printed on one side, or you can make one quickly out of an A4 sheet of paper.

Take an A4 sheet of paper. Draw a line from one corner to the diagonally opposite corner. Repeat this with the other two corners. This locates the centre of the A4 sheet (Step 1).

From the centre, draw a horizontal line and a vertical line. You now have four rectangles and a diagonal line running across them (Step 2).

Subdivide the rectangles again. You now have the centre of each rectangle. Draw a horizontal line and a vertical line through the centre point of each of these four smaller rectangles (Step 3).

You should now have a central rectangle that is the same proportions as your A1 sheet of paper. Cut out this rectangle and you have a window-mount with four measuring marks along the top, bottom and sides of the edges of the window (Step4).

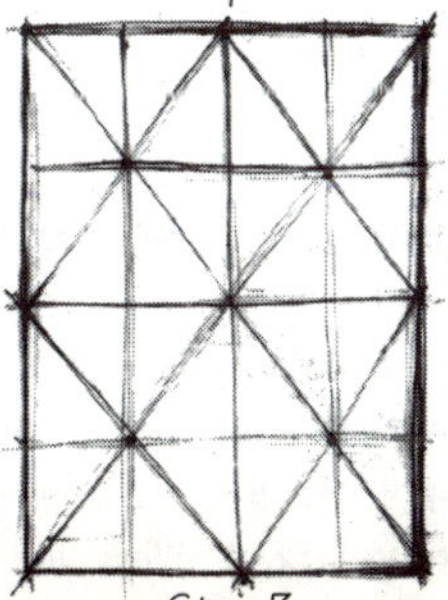

Step 3

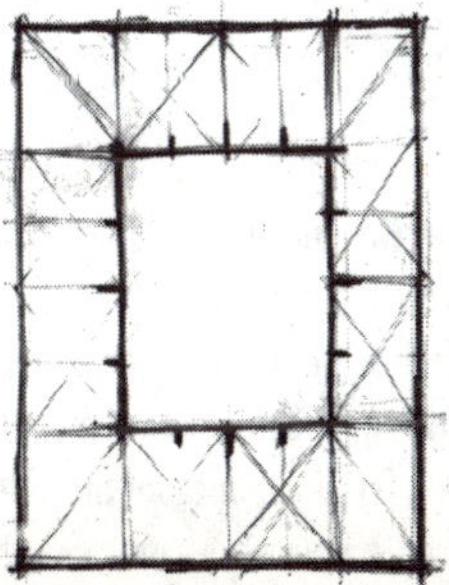

Step 4

POSITIONING THE EASEL

Position your easel in front of the set-up, about 1.5-2 m (5-6 ft) away. It should be placed at right angles to the still-life group so that your drawing board does not obscure your view. Ideally, if you are right-handed you should have your left side towards the still-life set-up, and vice versa for left-handed people. When you are happy with your position, draw around the feet of the easel so that if it moves accidentally, you can place it back in the same position. Attach A1 paper to your drawing board with masking tape.

You should stand for this type of drawing, so place your drawing board on the easel with your eye level approximately two-thirds of the way up the paper. Distortions occur while you draw, and if you sit throughout the drawing, you will not be in a position to spot them. If you stand up, you can move back from your drawing regularly to view it, and you will be able to see – and correct – distortions as they occur.

If you don't have access to an easel, prop up your drawing board against something like the back of a chair.

at your subject from exactly the same position. Some students prefer to attach the window-mount to the side of their drawing board.

Choose a composition that you find interesting. Do not have any objects going off the edge of the picture. In other words, only have complete objects in your composition.

The first mark

You are going to draw the non-object space (negative space). Think back to when you placed the table against the wall, creating a horizon line for the drawing. It is this line that you use to enter the drawing and assess the objects. Looking through the window-mount, see where the horizon line meets the inside edge of the mount on the left-hand side. Is it a quarter of the way up the side, or halfway up, or somewhere in between? When you have decided, place your charcoal in the corresponding position on the left side of your paper and begin to draw the horizon line. It is important at this point to find the angle of the line. Do not assume that it is horizontal from your viewpoint.

Draw this line with pressure until it meets the first object. Don't make it too light, as if you are afraid of it. Draw up and over the object, carefully assessing its silhouette and proportions. Look carefully as it is important that you observe the individual character of each object, noticing, for example, the lip around the top of a bottleneck. As the line proceeds over the top of the object and down the other side, it might hit another object. Your line must then change direction and follow the silhouette of that object. Otherwise, continue down the side of the first object until it comes to the horizon line again. Follow the horizon line until it meets the next object. Continue with this procedure until you reach the other side of your paper. In effect, you have drawn the top half of the objects in silhouette with one line that splits the paper in two (Step 1a).

Negative space and chiaroscuro: Steps 1a (below left), 1b (below right)

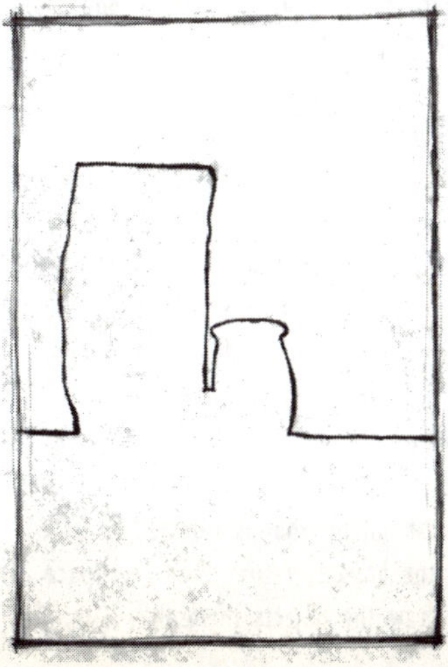

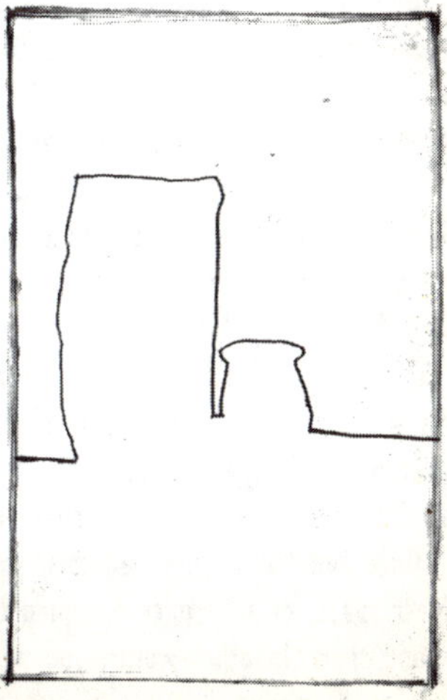

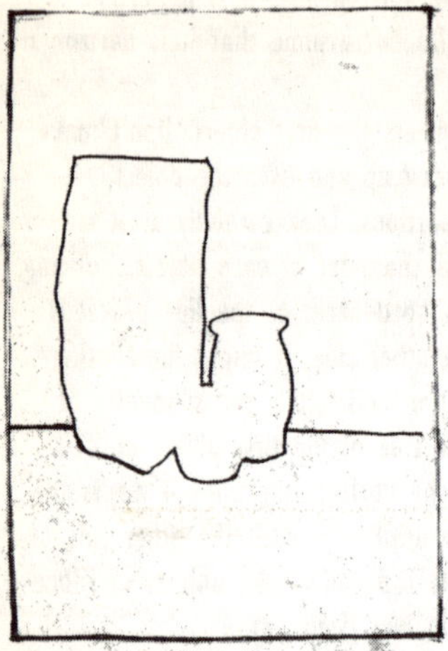

Step 2

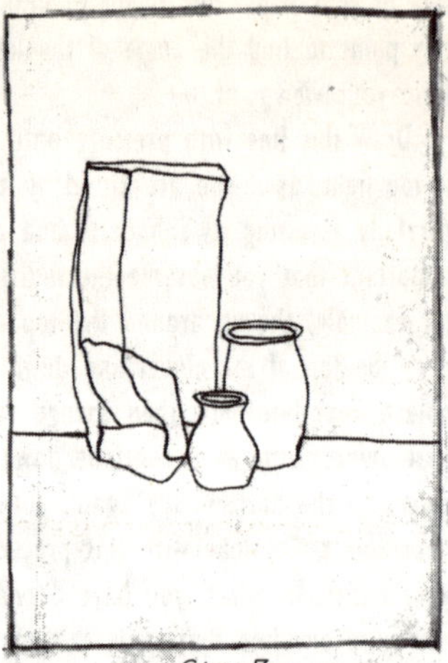

Step 3

Once you have done this, assess whether the objects look in proportion. A basic mistake made by some students is that they don't keep the horizon line at a consistent angle across the paper and the composition starts to become disjointed and distorted as a result (Step 1b).

For the next stage, place the charcoal on the point where you started the drawing, and retrace the first line until it meets the first object again. This time, follow around the lower silhouette of the objects. As with the top line, observe the objects carefully, measuring their relative proportions by sight. Continue this line until you reach the right-hand edge of the paper. This will give you three definite shapes: the shape of the wall in the background – negative space; the shape of the objects; and the shape of the table-top – also negative space (Step 2).

Once you have completed this, you can fill in what is referred to as the object space, or the space occupied by the objects, rather than the space around them. In other words, you now draw the objects themselves (Step 3).

It could be, at this point, that your drawing is slightly distorted or out of proportion. Don't worry, as this happens to most of us. Just persevere with the drawing and make the necessary adjustments.

Chiaroscuro

You now have the composition drawn out. Next, you need to set up a direct light source that provides contrasting tones – light lights and dark darks – across the group. A spotlight or an anglepoise lamp with a strong bulb are best. Try to cut out any other light source in the room (draw the curtains and turn off the overhead light) so that there is only one light source, which will make the lighting on the still life quite extreme and dramatic. Position the light to one side so that it is casting shadows across the objects from either right or left.

WORKING WITH THREE TONES

It can be difficult to distinguish between what is dark and what is not because we are presented with a lot of tonal transitions. The best way to sort this out is to make a scale consisting of three tones: black, grey, and the white of the paper for the lightest tone. Apply this scale to your observations by classifying each area of tone in the still life as one of these three tones (either very dark, a mid-tone or very light). If you think, for example, that something is nearly black, adopt it as being black. When the drawing has progressed sufficiently, you can introduce greater subtlety to the three tonal areas.

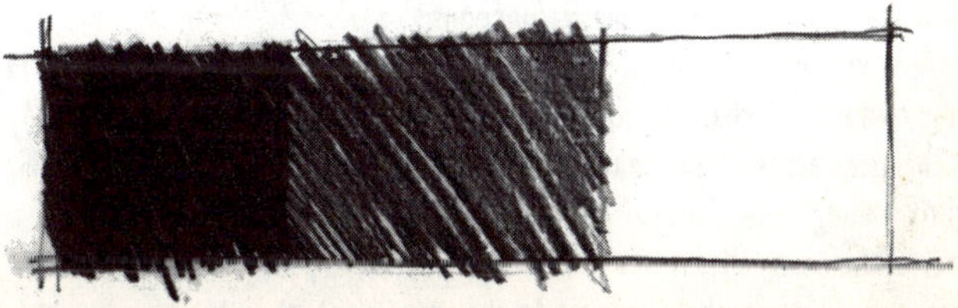

To emphasise the atmospheric, chiaroscuro effect that you are aiming to capture, squint your eyes as you look at the subject. This will obscure much of the detail and help you to see the subject as areas of tone. If you look at the group with your eyes fully open, they will adjust to the shadows and begin to pick out small details, which is not what you want. So, squinting your eyes, look at the group through the window-mount. Then, over the top of your original drawing, begin to draw the outlines of the shapes of the darkest areas.

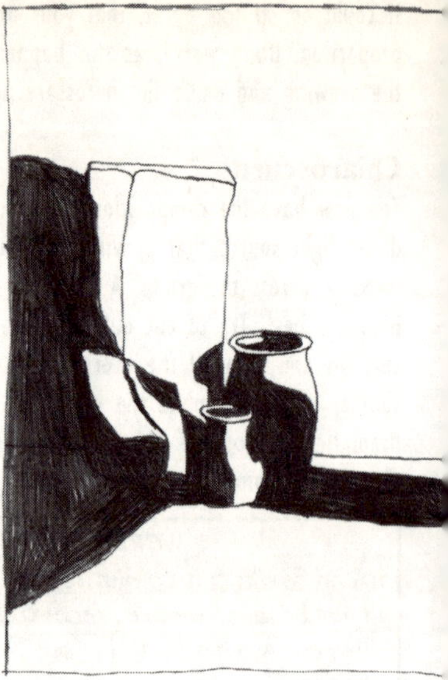

Step 4

A problem that tends to arise for students is that they want to remain truthful to the shape of the objects. This is definitely not what you should be seeking. Tones should be seen as areas that fall across objects, and the edges of objects may merge with shadows and become one area of tone. Don't worry about this loss of definition; objects will still be discernible because you are rendering them as the light affects them, and everyone is familiar with light and how it functions.

Once you have drawn in the outlines of the darkest areas, fill them in using compressed charcoal to produce a black and white drawing (Step 4).

The next stage is to create the grey areas. This is easy and enjoyable. Lightly smudge the charcoal all over the drawing with the flat of your hand, eliminating all the areas of white paper (Step 5). This creates mid-tones and an atmospheric effect. At the same time, the objects will recede

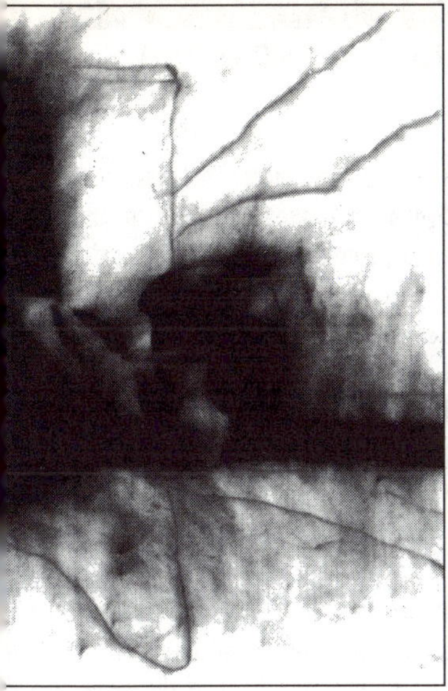

Step 5

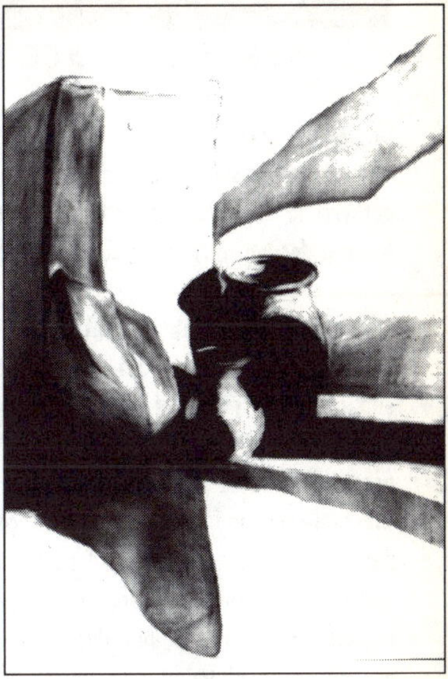

Step 6

into an illusory space. At this point you may need to re-establish the darker areas as the smudging will weaken them.

The final stage is to bring the white areas back. Do this by squinting at the subject in order to observe the lightest areas. Then use an eraser to establish the light areas in your drawing (Step 6).

Once you have completed these three tonal stages, you can become more subtle about the tonal changes. Observe the group with your eyes fully open so that you can see the subtler changes in tone that exist. When you have finished, you should have a dramatic, atmospheric, chiaroscuro drawing after the manner of Rembrandt.

Do a number of these drawings using a variety of simple compositions in order to build up your confidence.

PROJECT 2

NEGATIVE SPACE AND CHIAROSCURO

One 6-hour drawing

Materials: *still-life objects (see previous project), white sheet or paper for background, large sheet of black paper, spotlight or anglepoise lamp, window-mount, A1 cartridge paper, charcoal, compressed charcoal, eraser*

This project (see chapter frontispiece) uses the same techniques as the previous one, but your drawing skills will be extended, and this involves enhancing the group of objects and making the set-up more complex.

Place a table against the wall and cover it, and the wall behind if necessary, with a white sheet or piece of paper The next step is to make the table-top and background more complex. Take a large piece of black paper, tear it into strips, and stick the strips down on the backdrop and the table-top, thinking about the composition as you do so. Then place the objects on this set-up, but this time include more objects and create a greater depth of field. Some objects should be near the front of the table and can even overlap it. The light should be positioned in front and to one side of the table so that shadows are cast back across it at an angle.

Choose your composition carefully through the window-mount. When you are happy with it, begin drawing, as before, from the left-hand edge of the paper, following the horizon line and finding the objects above it. Then do the same for everything below the horizon line. Return to your starting point again and come back along the top line, picking up the places where the black paper establishes the vertical plane of the wall behind the table. Then do the same along the bottom line, establishing the horizontal plane of the table-top and picking up objects in that plane.

You need to measure the objects more accurately than you did in the previous project and locate them more carefully in relation to each other, but there are two things that will help you: measuring guides and vectors of analysis. If you have measuring guides or marks on the sides, top and bottom of your window-mount, dividing it into half and quarters, you will be able to locate each object's height and width in relation to these marks. Imagine that there is a grid across your viewing area.

Chiaroscuro

When you have established the composition, you can begin to think about tone. Position the light at the front and to one side, with the light falling diagonally across the set-up, so that the shadows imply planal recession across the table-top and a change of plane, or direction, on the wall. Think of the table-top as one plane (horizontal) and the wall behind as another plane (vertical). The black shadows travel back across the table towards the wall, and in some cases up it. When you add these shadows to your drawing, they will indicate receding space and a large depth of field.

> *VECTORS OF ANALYSIS*
>
> *A helpful observational technique, which can be used in conjunction with measuring guides on a window-mount, is to use what are known as vectors of analysis. A vector is a direction. Take the direction of a line, for example on the side of an object, and extend it. Such a line will often pick up on a line on another object in another part of the composition. This creates a relationship and a point of contact between the two objects.*

Continue as before, drawing in the outlines of the darkest tones, remembering to squint your eyes to simplify the tones. Draw all the dark areas. Students are often confused at this stage by the black paper. The areas of black paper in shadow will be black, but where it is lit, these areas will appear grey. Tone depends on the amount of light falling on that area: white surfaces could become dark tonal areas if they are in dark shadow, and black surfaces become a mid grey where they are strongly lit. What you have to remember is that you are looking at the effects of light.

Continue as in the previous project, developing the dark, mid-toned and light areas, until you have a very strong, atmospheric, spatial drawing.

CHAPTER 2

TEXTURE

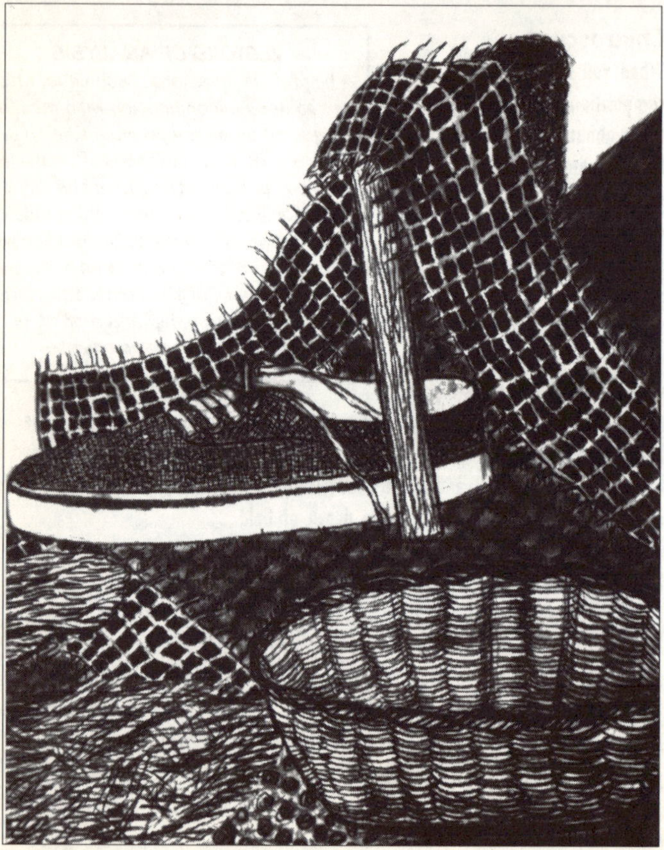

Space, form, light and atmosphere in a subject are not the only concerns that occupy artists. The challenge, conscious or not, of creating a sense of touch through visual illusion, whatever the subject matter, has also always excited artists. From grandiose objects made of gold or silver to the everyday earthenware pot, or from a peach to a cabbage, the depiction of texture has been a liberating area of work for the artist. It has allowed them to experiment with their medium and to show off their abilities. Moreover, the implied suggestion of texture and surface qualities did not align itself with politics, academic ideas or movements. It is what it is.

In the past, texture was as important to artists in the classical tradition as it was to those working in a more romantic or naturalistic way. Whatever school or background they came from, they all imbued their objects with the idea of surface qualities. However, these qualities have been treated with different degrees of intensity. While some artists slavishly labour over the minutest textural details, others can just as well imply these qualities with a sublime simplicity using a few statements or marks. Whatever approach is taken, the illusion of texture can be exciting both for the artist to create and for the viewer to perceive.

Texture is a very important element in our visual understanding of the world and it is appropriate in drawing at any level. It can be executed as a labour of love or put in as a mere suggestion, but however it is presented it is understood by all. We know and understand immediately what the artist is trying to convey.

There are many examples of work concerned with texture, not only in still life but in most other subject areas, too. Look at still-life drawings that convey texture, but also look at art using other subject matter, such as landscapes and interiors, and using other mediums, too. Because paint is a medium that particularly lends itself to this approach, there are many more paintings than drawings available that describe texture

PROJECT 1

MARK-MAKING

One 2-hour drawing

Materials: *A1 cartridge paper, charcoal, compressed charcoal, eraser*

The aim is to depict your sense of touch through your visual sense.

First of all, you must become familiar with your drawing equipment, which in this case is charcoal and an eraser. In order to discover the ways in which these drawing tools can be used for describing texture, fill a sheet of paper with a vast range of different types of marks using charcoal and eraser. In doing this you will be starting to build up a vocabulary of mark-making that you can refer to later, when drawing textural objects. Try not to be obvious with the way you make marks. Be inventive and try using your eraser over the marks to push them or reduce them.

Be aware of the different ways in which you can hold the charcoal to make marks. Try using the side of the charcoal, pulling it down the paper to make a sharp line. Then try dragging it across the paper sideways. If you need to get a sharp, thin edge, snap the charcoal in two. Marks can be intuitive, like scribbles, to describe an organic type of texture, or they can be regular and systematic, creating a sense of order and regularity that can depict man-made textures.

Right: Examples of mark-making

Try making marks in the following ways: straight, harsh marks; fluid marks; stabbing marks; caressing marks; thick marks; thin marks; circular marks; triangular marks; light marks; dark marks; unconscious marks; conscious marks. Don't just stick to these suggestions; add some of your own ways and types of marks. You will be amazed at what you can achieve within the limitations of charcoal and eraser. Save this sheet as reference for future drawings.

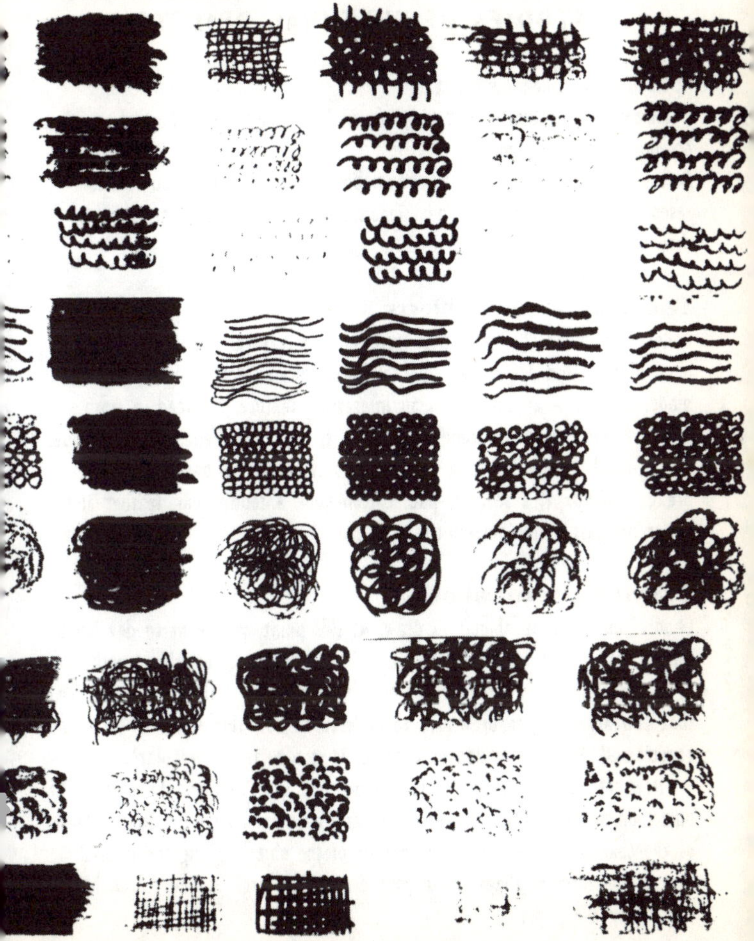

PROJECT 2

STUDIES OF TEXTURAL OBJECTS

Approximately 1/2 hour per object

Materials: *textural objects and surfaces, A1 cartridge paper, charcoal, compressed charcoal, eraser*

Before engaging in a concentrated and complex drawing of texture, you need to research the idea in order to gain an understanding of what it is you are about to draw and what you are trying to achieve.

Selecting textural objects

Collect a number of objects that have varying textural qualities. You will need objects that are rough, smooth, hard, soft, reflective, dull, furry, man-made, natural – anything with an interesting texture. Seaweed, a worn piece of wood, a rough stone or brick, a sponge, polythene, string or rope, a mop-head, coarse fabric, a dish cloth, a straw hat, a basket, shells, bread, a bandage, a scouring-pad, cotton-wool, a teddy bear, leather and paper are just a few possibilities.

Drawing a textural object

Choose one of these objects to draw. At this point, you want to develop a feeling for, or a sense of, your object. Handle your chosen object with your eyes closed and be very aware of how it feels, as it is this sense of touch that you are going to draw. Try to understand how the object is constructed. Is it man-made or organic? Is it regular or irregular?

Now set up the background (see 'Space and Light', Project 1), placing the object on a white table-top with your easel positioned near by. Take a piece of charcoal and quickly draw the outline of the object, giving the general idea of the form or shape. Make your drawing as large as you reasonably can, filling the paper.

The next step is to understand and analyse the texture of the object. You are not going to draw this object in minute detail. The intention is to understand the structure of the object and how the structure contributes to its texture. At the same time, think about how you can simulate the texture through marks made with the charcoal – making visual marks that tell us what that object is made of, marks that are a metaphor for that texture. For instance, if you are drawing a block of wood, you do not need to copy every grain that you can see on it; you should try to imply the grain.

There is no mystery to this way of drawing, and the approach can be quite graphic. If you cannot think how to imply the grain of wood, think about the quite simple way in which wood grain would be indicated in a cartoon or comic book and use this as a starting point. A block of wood could first be drawn to show its form – i.e., that it is a three-dimensional object. It can then be turned into a wooden block by implying the grain of the wood. Where the grain goes over the edge of the block, the change in direction of the grain is followed. This gives the illusion of the texture of wood, and the change in direction over the form also gives an understanding of the form.

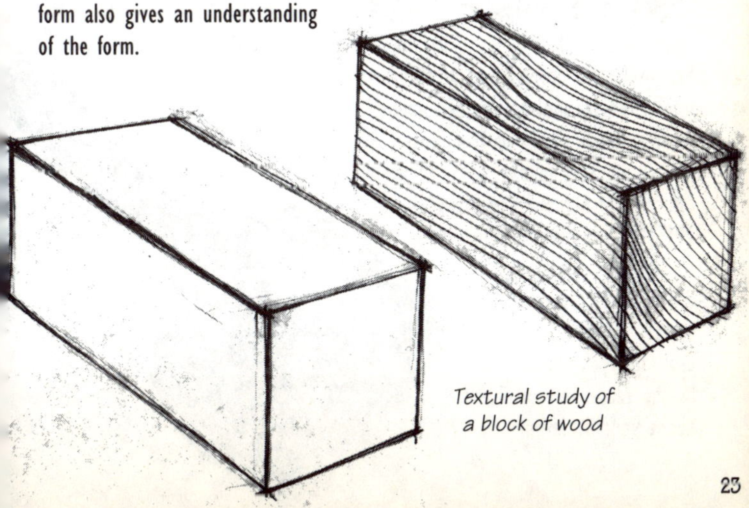

Textural study of a block of wood

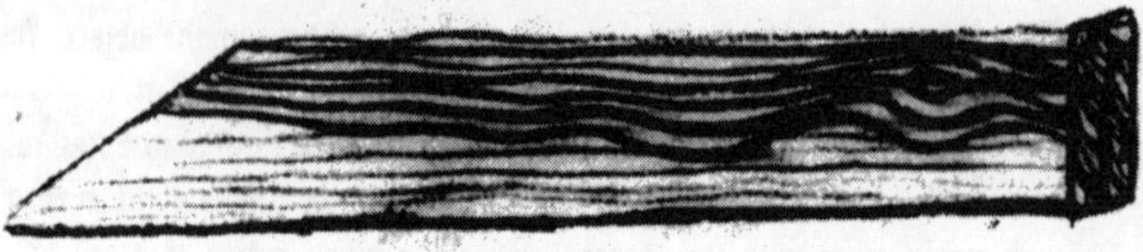

Above and below: Textural studies of objects

Once you have an understanding of a particular texture and a way of implying it, you can draw that texture without necessarily looking at it any more because you have created a metaphor, or language, for it and all you have to do is implement it. Remember, however, that the process can be very quick (if you are drawing cotton-wool, for instance), or it can be very concentrated and lengthy (if you are drawing something like a wicker basket), depending on the subject. Look at the drawings of Leonardo da Vinci (1452-1519), which include both very beautiful close observations of nature (flowers, roots and so on), and interesting textural studies of running water. Look, too, at the studies and drawings of Max Ernst (1891-1976), who was a master at using texture. Some of the object drawings of Fernand Léger (1881-1955) are also worth studying.

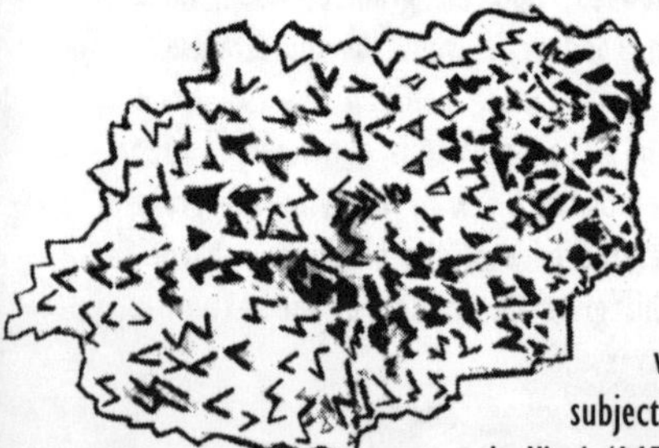

Do several drawings of different textural objects. After a few drawings, you should be feeling reasonably confident about your achievements.

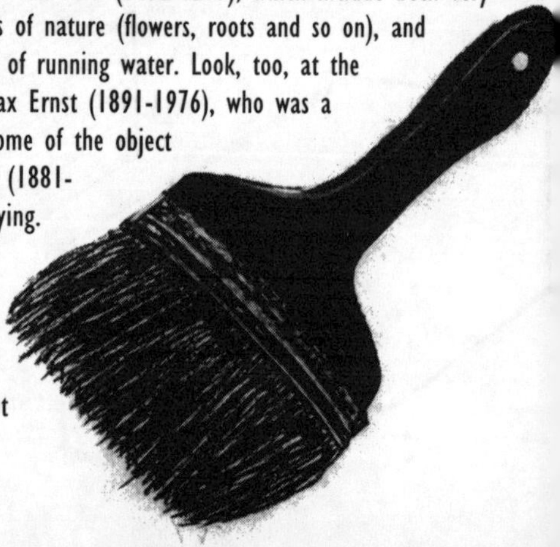

PROJECT 3
FROTTAGE

A few minutes for each drawing

Materials: *textural surfaces, thin paper such as newsprint, charcoal, compressed charcoal*

Frottage creates an impression, in charcoal, of the surface over which the charcoal is rubbed. For example, if you try frottage using a wooden floorboard, you will get an impression of the surface of the wood. Use thin paper (try newsprint, which is a cheap paper available from good art shops) and make rubbings of as many different textured surfaces as you can find, both indoors and outdoors.

Examples of frottage

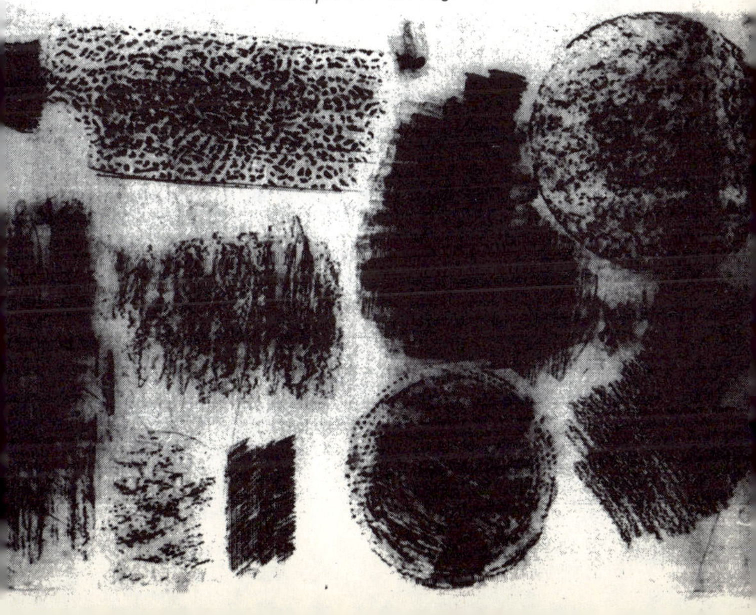

Suitable surfaces

Stable surfaces are best for this project. For example, you can try frottage on a variety of walls, a variety of floors, pavements, grating, fences, drain covers and so on. Experiment with many different surfaces (soft and hard) and see what results you get.

Frottage should help you with your own ideas about mark-making and will help you to build up your own vocabulary of textural marks.

PROJECT 4

TEXTURAL STILL LIFE

One 6-hour drawing, including setting up

Materials: *textural objects (see Project 2), textured surface or fabric, A1 cartridge paper, window-mount, charcoal, compressed charcoal, eraser*

You are now going to embark on a textural still-life drawing, but first you need to set up a suitable arrangement. By now, you will probably have collected a certain number of objects, but as you become more familiar with the idea of texture you will probably have other ideas about what you want to draw. So now might be a good time to collect a few more objects.

Setting up a textural still life

Push a table flush against the wall (see 'Space and Light', Project 1), and over the top place something that covers the whole surface to give an underlying texture on which to place the objects. A candlewick bedspread is good because it has a loose texture, yet it also has a structure. Place your objects on this, laying some of them side by side and scattering others on top of each other. Remember that adjacent objects should contrast with

Right: Textural still life

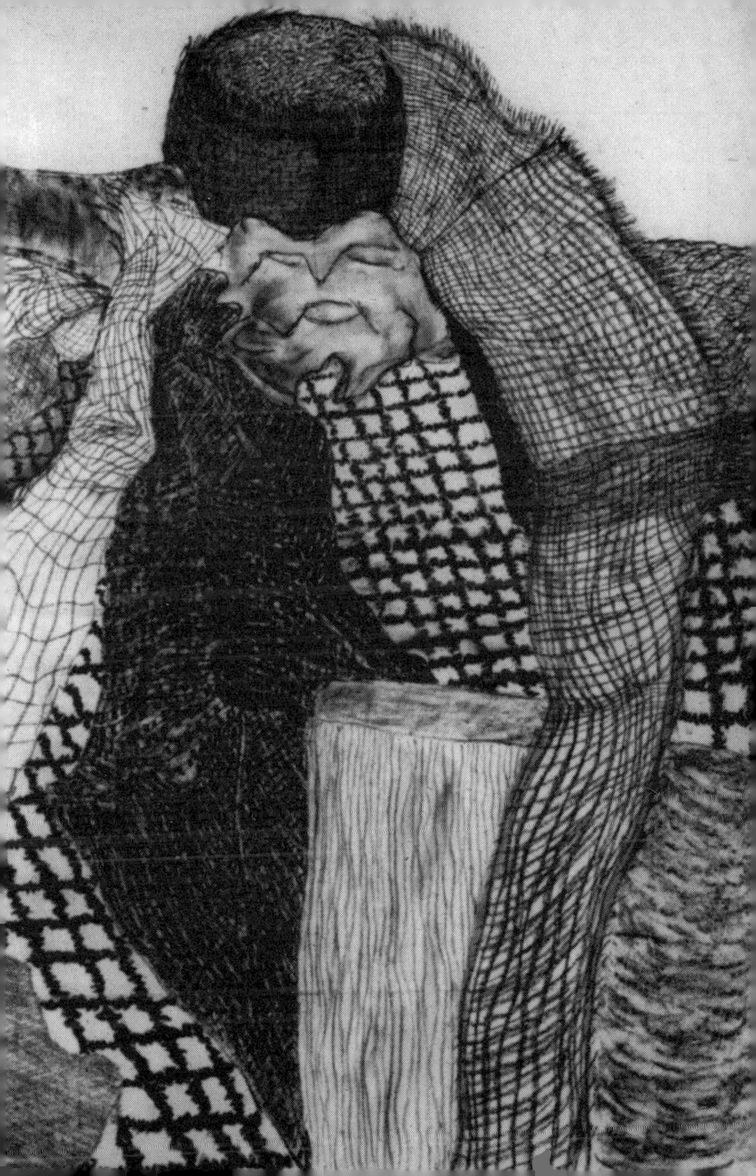

Don't draw one object in isolation and then move on to another object in a different part of the set-up. Build up your drawing gradually by working on one area, and then moving to a contrasting texture next to it until you have completed your drawing.

each other in texture and tone if possible, so try not to put similar textures next to each other or the drawing will become confusing.

Starting to draw

Use the window-mount to select your composition. As this is a complex and concentrated drawing, do not attempt to draw the whole arrangement. Choose a section of the group that offers you a simple yet exciting contrast of textures. Be prepared to move objects around until you find a satisfactory composition.

Start by finding the outline of the objects and draw them as they relate to each other. You can use negative space and horizontal and vertical lines (see 'Space and Light', Project 1) to help with the measurement and placement of objects in relation to each other. This will help you to construct the basic composition for the drawing. When you have completed this stage, you can begin to draw the textures.

Remember to refer back to your previous textural drawings and frottage for ideas. Also, have a spare piece of paper at hand to experiment with different ways of drawing textures as you go along. The negative texture – the surface on which the objects are lying – is just as important as the textures of the objects themselves.

CHAPTER 3

FUNDAMENTAL FORM

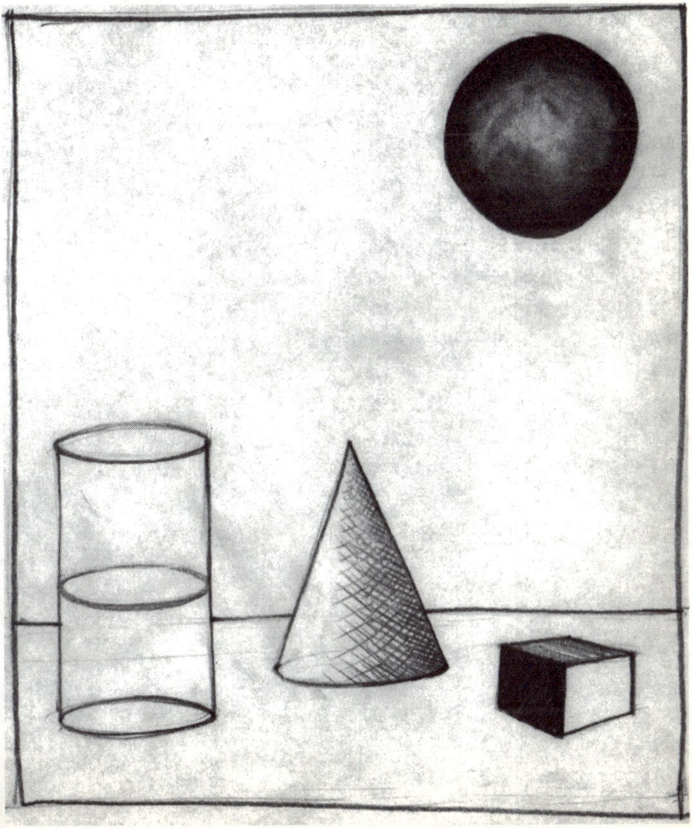

In this chapter we will look at the illusion of three-dimensions (form) on a two-dimensional surface (a flat piece of paper). First, however, it is essential to understand what is meant by the term 'form'. Many people confuse the idea of form with the idea of shape; people often refer to shape when they really mean form. Shape is flat and two-dimensional and is bound by a perimeter, whereas form has volume and is three-dimensional. In early Byzantine paintings, artists would top-light the heads of saints and paint the figures with limited or no space behind them. This created a sense of form as relief, like a relief carving. Approaches to describing the three-dimensional nature of things gradually developed from the relief into the depiction of fully three-dimensional forms in more naturalistic or constructed spaces.

When we draw from observation, we are creating the illusion of form. This can be achieved in many ways, but, like all aspects of drawing, it is only a part of the whole subject of still life. In fact, without particularly focusing on form, we have touched on it in the previous two chapters. In Chapter 1, the use of chiaroscuro provided an understanding of objects existing in space and consequently suggested a three-dimensional world. In Chapter 2 we looked at the way in which the texture of an object can help to show the form of that object.

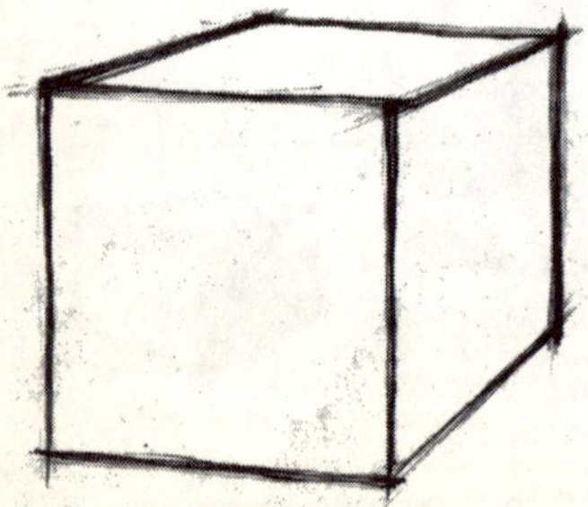

Cube

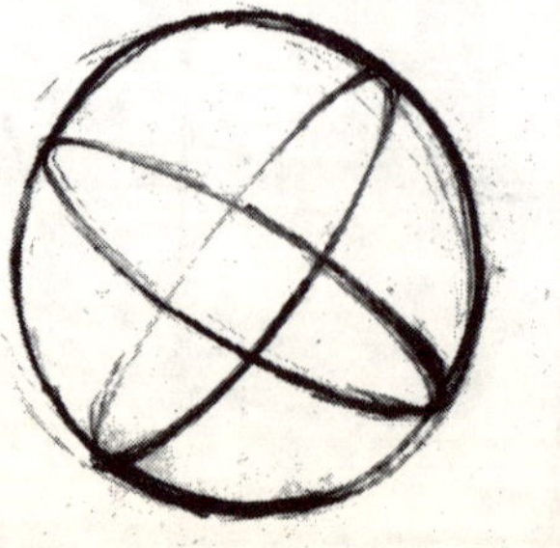

Sphere

DRAWING WITH FUNDAMENTAL FORMS

There are countless numbers of different organic (natural) and geometric shapes and forms, but the drawing methods in the following projects make use of four fundamental forms: the cube, the sphere, the cone and the cylinder.

How do we go about creating the illusion of form through drawing? The usual way is by observing and analysing the subject in terms of the underlying fundamental form or forms. You can then draw the basic form of the object as a cube, sphere, cylinder or cone, or a combination of any of these, modifying or emphasising this where necessary. Some objects are quite simple to categorise, whereas others offer a choice and you will have to decide which will work best. This method of working enables you to break down the complex visual world into simple units that you can then embellish as necessary.

Once you have decided which fundamental form your object is based on, you can use one of a number of drawing techniques to demonstrate your understanding of that form.

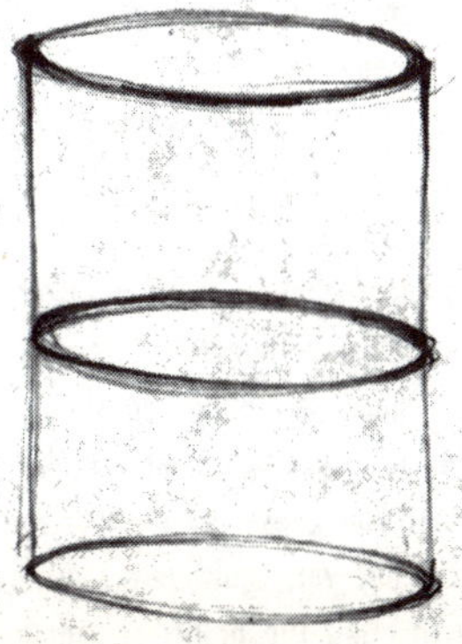

Cylinder

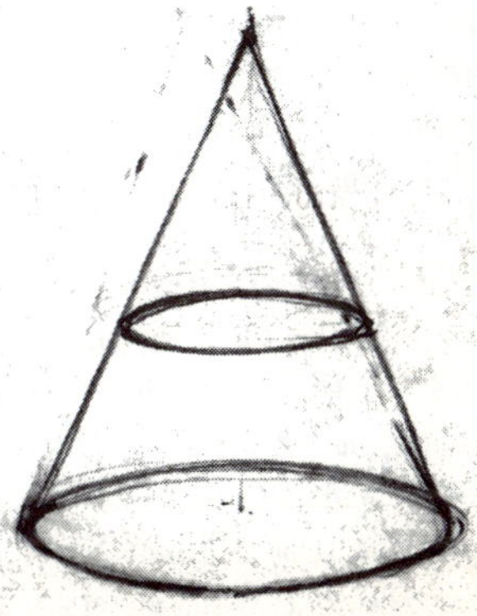

Cone

Before starting, you may find it helpful to practise drawing ellipses and the four fundamental forms from different angles (without using perspective). For instance, try drawing a cube from above, below, side view and so on.

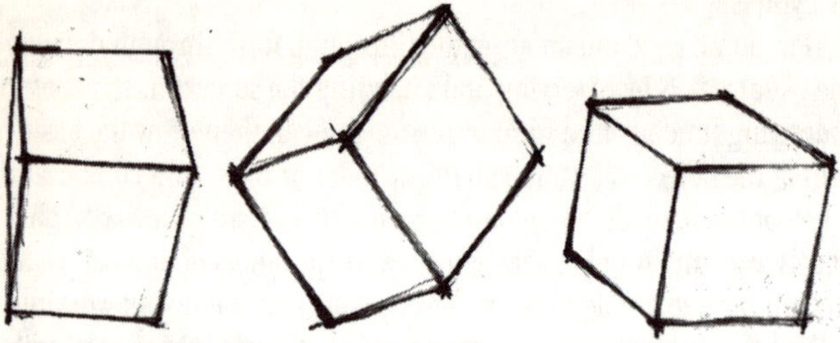

PROJECT 1

THREE TECHNIQUES FOR DEMONSTRATING FORM

Three 3-hour drawings

Materials: *still-life objects, window-mount, 4 sheets of A1 cartridge paper, 2-3 sheets of paper for practising, 2B and 3B pencils, eraser*

This project looks at three simple ways – cross-sectional analysis, modelling with tone and crosshatching – to denote fundamental form.

Set up a table against a wall and create a plain backdrop. Then select a number of objects. At this stage, do not choose any items with very complicated or difficult forms, but equally do not choose anything too simple. For example, do not use a straightforward cube or cylinder, but select objects that are variations on these. The objects that you chose for the projects in 'Space and Light' will probably do very well, but you could select different things. Construct a still-life group, bearing in mind the points raised in that chapter about the placement of objects.

Cross-sectional analysis

Set up your easel with drawing board and paper. Hold up your window-mount towards the still-life group and select your composition. Using pencil, proceed to draw the negative space and the object space (see 'Space and Light' Project 1), filling the A1 sheet. You will end up with a drawing that consists of shape, not form. Now analyse and draw the objects by breaking them down into their fundamental forms.

To emphasise the forms, draw with line around and through each object, known as cross-sectional analysis, which will give the illusion of three dimensions. Imagine that the objects you are drawing are transparent and that you are drawing the line onto the actual objects and can see it following the form round each object. Once you have drawn all the objects in this way, you can add subtle details about the form to each object.

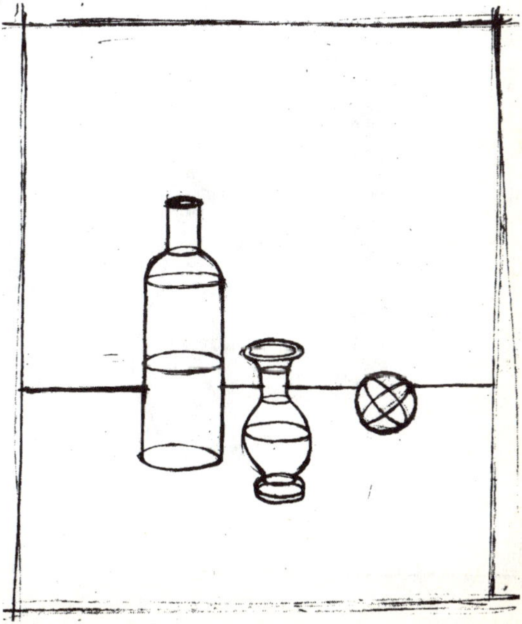

Cross-sectional analysis

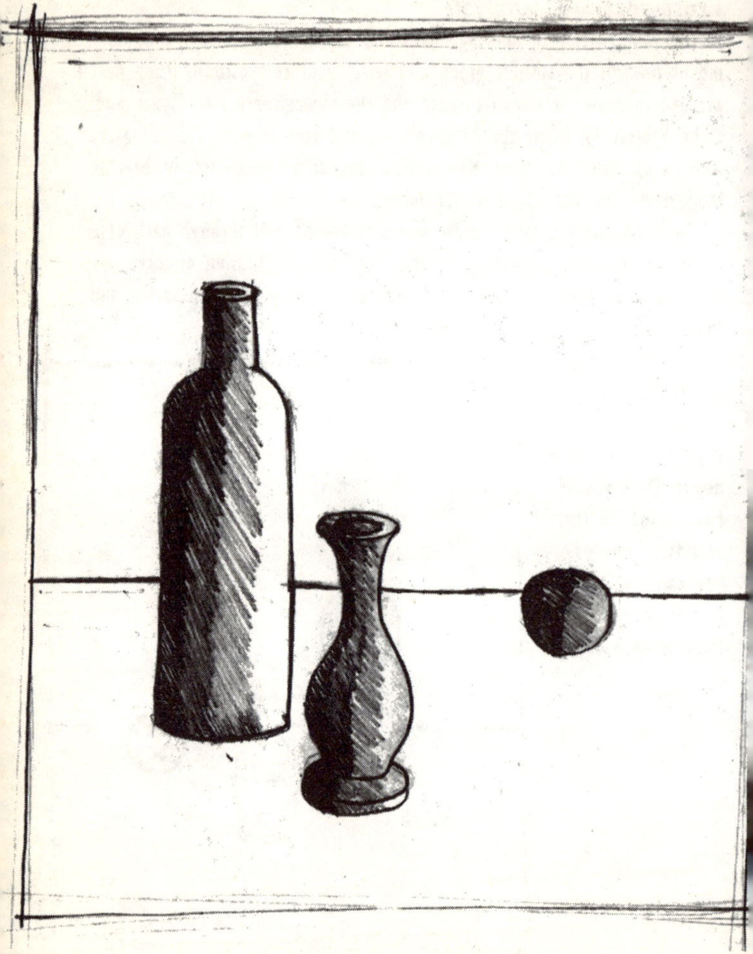

Modelling form with tone

Modelling form using tone

The human eye does not see a line around an object, but what we do see are areas of tone. Line is constructed by us in drawing: when drawing the outline of an object, we are not drawing a line that we see; we are inventing a line to denote the edge of something. When modelling with tone, we create the illusion of volume by using gradations of tone around the form. Before trying to model form using tone, try creating four different tones with pencil and eraser on a spare piece of paper. Make the darkest tone black and the lightest the white of the paper, and then make two different grey tones. As an exercise, try drawing the fundamental forms using tone.

Next, set yourself up with a new sheet of A1 paper. Hold your window-mount up towards the still-life group and select your composition. Using pencil, draw the negative space and the object space, making sure to fill your sheet of paper. The next step is to model the forms with tone, with either a real or imaginary, direct light source falling on them.

When drawing using chiaroscuro, you were drawing light and shade, or areas of different tones, without regard to the edges of objects. When using tone to model form, however, you do need to draw the edges of objects, drawing what you know to exist and using tone to depict the object as three-dimensional. The emphasis, when you are modelling with tone, should be on giving the illusion of form, as opposed to chiaroscuro, where the emphasis is on drawing light and shade, the form of the object being secondary to the tone.

Next, using another sheet of A1 paper, make another drawing of the same composition using just tone and no outlines.

Crosshatching

Take a new sheet of A1 paper and make another drawing of the set-up using negative space and cross-sectional analysis. You can use the same composition or a new one. In this drawing, you are going to use cross-hatching rather than tonal modelling to describe the forms. Crosshatching

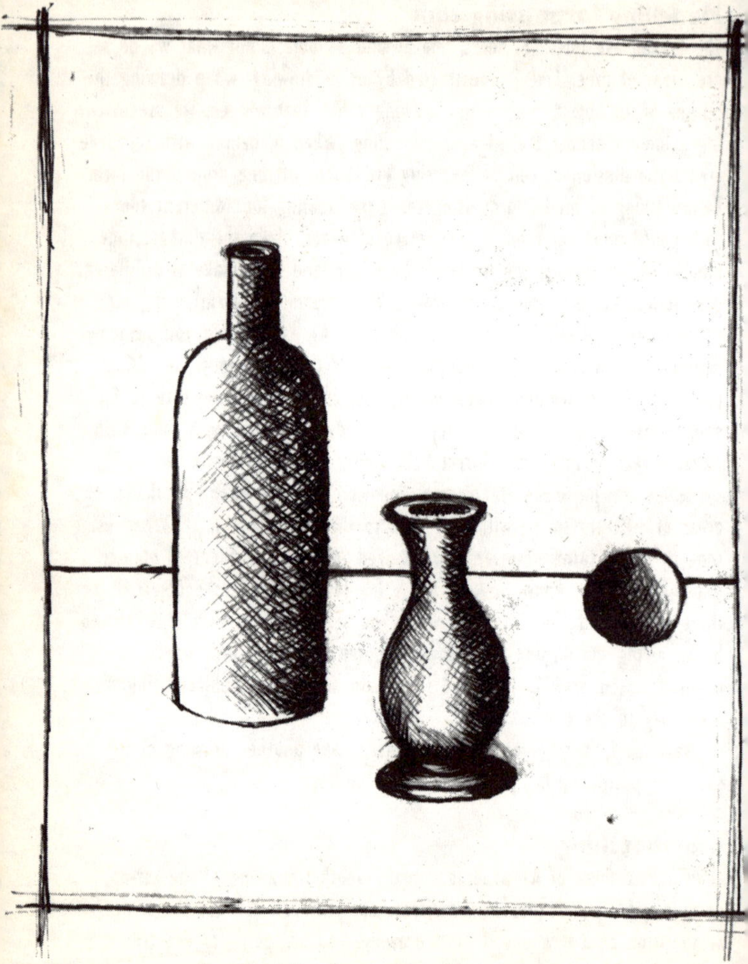

Modelling form with crosshatching

consists of a series of crisscross lines that can be used to emphasise the form through tonal variation. In some of his etchings Pablo Picasso (1881-1973) used crosshatching, but he let the crisscross lines evolve almost into a scribble. Both regular and scribbly crosshatching work on the principle of creating different tones through the density of the crosshatching.

The difference between crosshatching and modelling with tone is that modelling with tone is based more closely on observation and is more often used to create gradual transitions in tone. This is because we can actually see tonal variations. Crosshatching, on the other hand, is a purely invented mark; it is not something we see when looking at objects.

Because crosshatching is artificial and constructed, it does not necessarily rely on a directional light source. However, it does rely on a certain amount of observation and an understanding of form. Also, it can be constructed in a way that is not consistent with any particular light source (imagined or real). For example, within a still-life drawing each object could be treated as if lit by a different light source from a different direction. And despite this, the whole drawing can still function as an illusion of space and form.

Additionally, modelling with tone can be used in a similar way to crosshatching (that is, in a more artificial and invented way), and crosshatching can be used observationally.

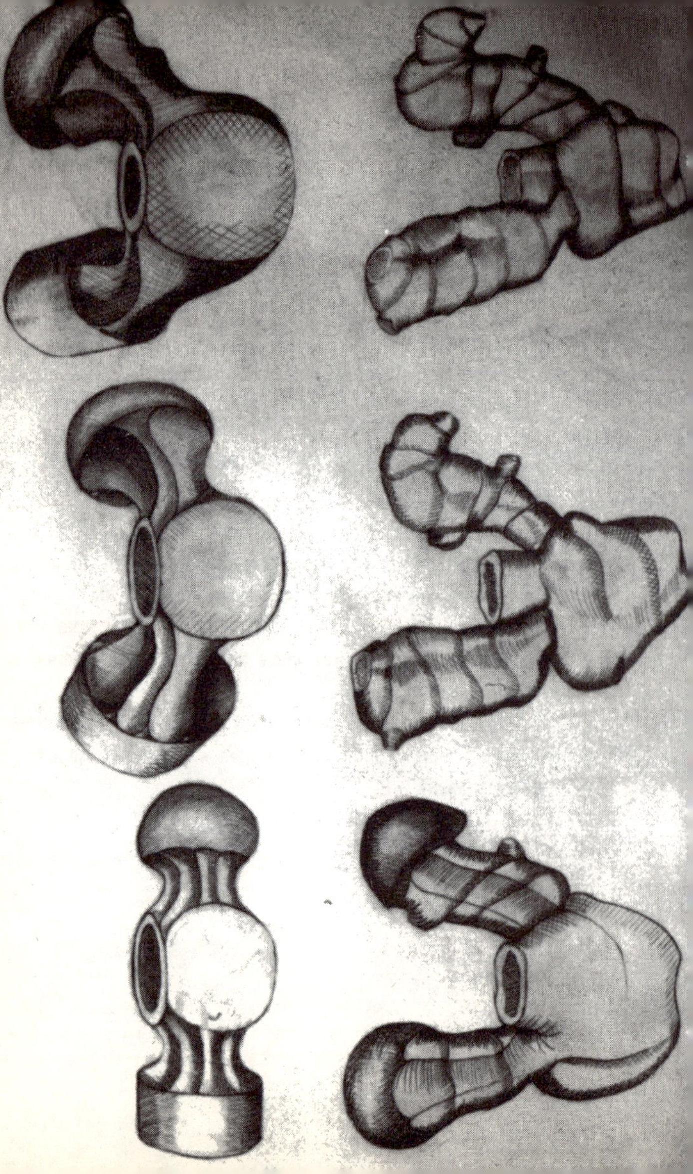

PROJECT 2
METAMORPHOSIS

Six 1-hour drawings

Materials: *2 objects, A1 cartridge paper, 2B and 3B pencils, eraser*

Using one of the techniques from the previous project, make a series of drawings in which one object gradually metamorphoses into another.

For this project you need to select two different forms. One must be a geometric, man-made object and the second a natural object with an organic form, but there must be some harmony and connection between the two. In other words, do not choose objects with opposing forms. As an example, you could choose a garlic press and a daffodil. Although very different, these two objects both have a kind of stem with a type of head attached to it, and one could evolve into the other through a series of drawings.

Remember to break the objects down into their fundamental forms to give yourself a much clearer understanding of the objects.

Take a sheet of A1 paper and divide it into six equal squares. Decide which technique you are going to use out of cross-sectional analysis, modelling with tone or crosshatching, and draw one of your objects in the top left-hand corner. Then draw the other object in the bottom right-hand corner using the same technique. Then proceed to do a series of four more drawings, using your chosen technique and working from the top left corner to the bottom right, gradually transforming one object into the other.

Try this project two more times, using each of the other techniques described in the previous project. You can use the same objects or choose different ones.

Left: Metamorphosis in six stages

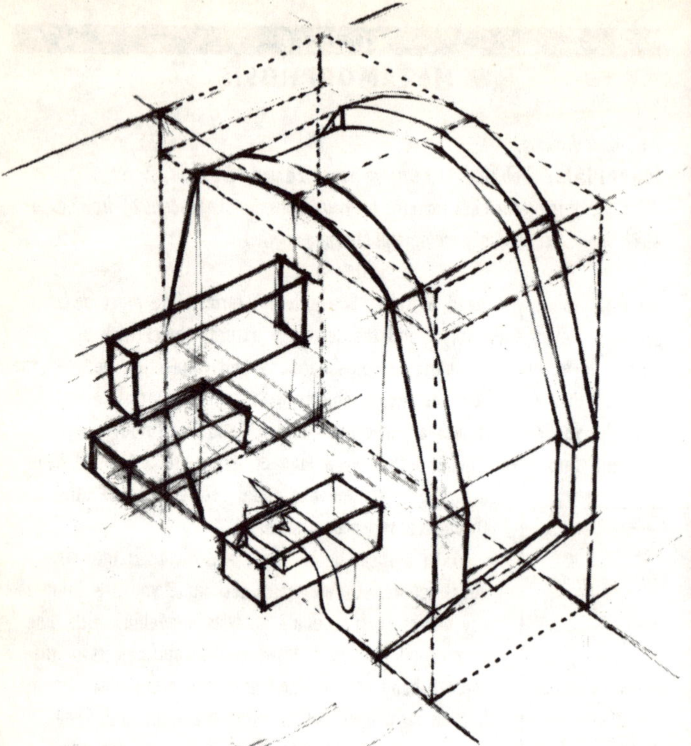

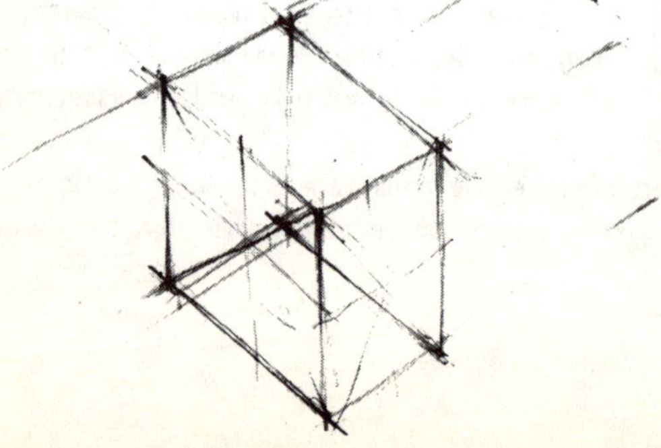

The plug is constructed from a box or crate.

PROJECT 3

PARALLEL PROJECTION AND EXPLODED DIAGRAMMATIC DRAWINGS

One 3-hour drawing and one 6-hour drawing

Materials: *1 object, 2 sheets of A1 cartridge paper, 2B and 3B pencils, eraser*

This project consists of two drawings – a parallel projection drawing and an exploded diagrammatic drawing – that show how an object is constructed. This type of drawing is usually reserved for instructions on how to assemble technical objects and for instructional diagrams in car manuals. However, if you can develop an understanding of this working method, it will improve your grasp of form. And although these approaches are not obvious means of expression, it is possible to use them in that way.

You need to choose an object with certain attributes. It must be fairly simple, constructed from a number of pieces, and you must be able to take it apart, which probably means that it will be man-made and functional. An electric plug is used as an example here, but you can choose anything that appeals to you as long as it fits the criteria above.

Parallel projection drawing

Using fundamental form and cross-sectional analysis (see Project 1), draw the object from a three-quarter view (meaning that you can see two sides and the top plane) using a parallel projection; that is, you are not drawing it in perspective. All lines that recede into the distance remain the same distance apart (i.e., parallel). Make the drawing quite large, filling your A1 paper, because it is easier to recognise your mistakes at this scale. This stage of the drawing will help your initial understanding of the object.

Left: Parallel projection drawing of an electric plug

Exploded diagrammatic drawing

In this drawing the approach is to disassemble the object visually using a parallel projection, so that the finished drawing shows the dismantled components of the object.

In the case of the plug, it is again drawn within a crate or box, but this time the crate is projected forwards, altering its dimensions. It is important to keep the crate in proportion to your object on the front elevation: imagine what type of crate your object would fit into and draw it accordingly. If you are drawing a tall, thin object don't draw a small, squat crate; draw a tall crate but, as mentioned above, make the crate longer than the object. This will help you to position each component so that it looks like an integral part of the object, and to see how the pieces relate to the object as a whole when they are disassembled and projected forwards.

Now take your object apart so that you can study each component individually and set it in the framework of the overall drawing. If you are drawing a plug, first take the back part and draw it at the back of the crate, using the crate as a guideline. Also draw the internal parts (Step 1).

The next step is to project forwards within

Step 3

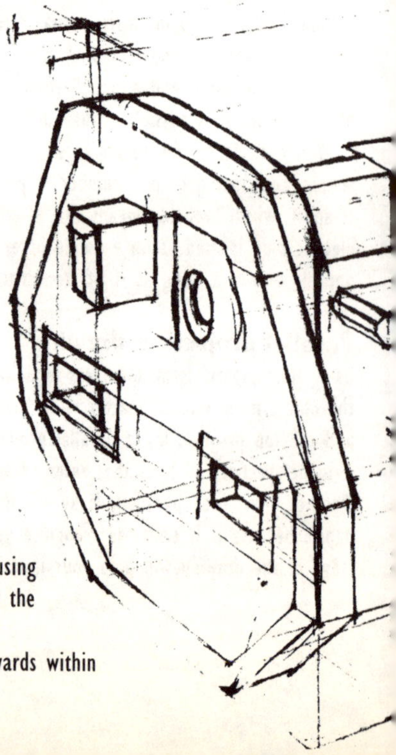

the framework, using the guidelines of the crate, and draw the three brass fingers and the fuse casing (Step 2). For the final step, using the same projection, place the top of the plug at the other end of the crate, again using the crate as a guide to its correct position (Step 3).

Try this approach with a number of drawings of similar objects.

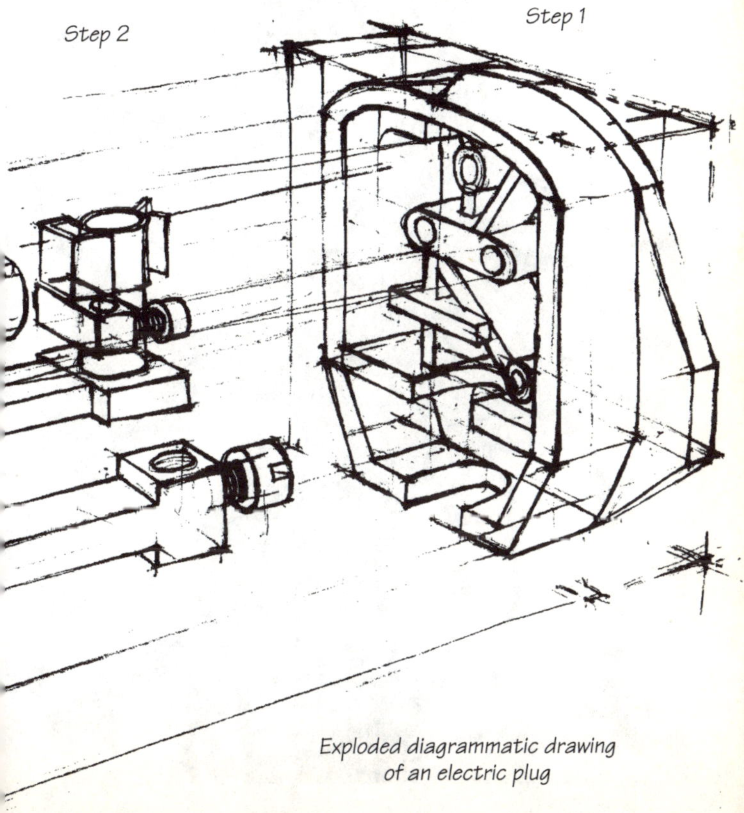

Exploded diagrammatic drawing of an electric plug

CHAPTER 4

DRAPERY

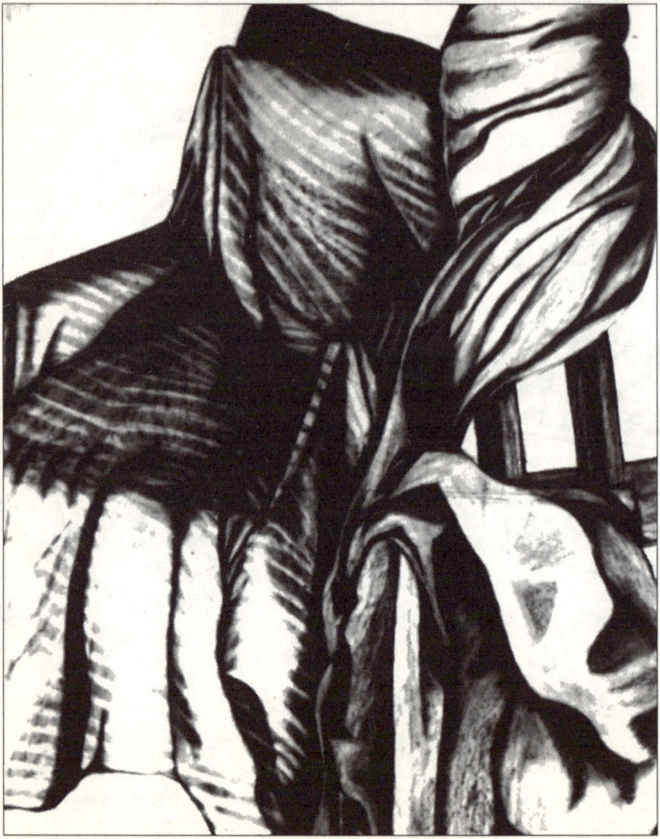

The term 'drapery' refers to the artistic arrangement of clothing or material in painting, sculpture and drawing. Drapery has been used as still-life subject matter in drawing for centuries. In the past, artists' apprentices would spend hours producing drawings of drapery as part of their training. It became such an essential part of art, particularly for commissioned portraits of statesmen or wealthy merchants, that some artists began to specialise in it. The master would paint the portrait and then employ the drapery artist to finish the background and finery. Of the many examples of drapery studies that exist, those by Leonardo da Vinci, in particular, are worth looking at. However, bear in mind that although important, drapery and clothing were usually secondary to the main subject and supported the anecdotal content of the work.

Another traditional use of drapery is in trompe l'oeil – the creation of an illusion of real drapery in a real setting. For example, a curtain would be painted onto a wall with a landscape painted beyond it, and at first glance they would appear to be a real curtain and a real landscape. Drapery is used in this case as a transitional device for moving from reality to illusion.

Drapery has often been used by artists as a compositional device, to create the underlying structure of a painting. In fact, in some cases its compositional function was so blatant that it bore no relation to naturalism but was purely a pictorial construct. Nicolas Poussin (1593/4-1665), Jan Vermeer (1632-75) and El Greco (1541-1614) used drapery as a device, but each in a different way. Poussin manipulated drapery in order to help the compositional flow in his paintings and guide the eye across the picture so that it creates movement across the picture plane, while at the same time echoing the lines of moving figures. Vermeer, like Poussin, used drapery as a compositional device. In contrast to Poussin and Vermeer, El Greco painted drapery very expressively, so that it flows through the picture space with a sense of monumentality and purpose. Yet drapery in El Greco's paintings still has the desired effect of guiding and encouraging the eye through and across the picture space.

The following projects focus on clothing and drapery because they are useful subject matter on which to practise creating the illusion of form and texture. You will be combining methods of drawing covered in previous chapters.

PROJECT 1

TROMPE L'OEIL

One 5-hour drawing

Materials: *an article of clothing or drapery, a very large sheet of drawing paper, spotlight or anglepoise lamp, a range of graphite sticks and pencils, or charcoal and compressed charcoal, plastic eraser*

Choosing drapery

Because this drawing deals with tone, you need to select the drapery item carefully. Choose something like a black or white shirt or coat. Also give some consideration to the texture of the garment, as you can use this to enhance the drawing. For instance, a shirt might have a lace collar and cuffs. A black leather jacket would make a very good subject as the dense tone of the leather, the creases and zips all make for an interesting drawing. If lack of space is a problem, you could use a small item such as a scarf or towel.

Setting up the still life

As with previous drawings, the still-life arrangement is very important. If you have chosen a shirt, coat or something similar, place it on a hanger and hang it flat against the wall from a nail or hook. If you have chosen something like a scarf or towel, hang it directly on a hook or nail. It is also important that the background is neutral in tone (that is, white or a

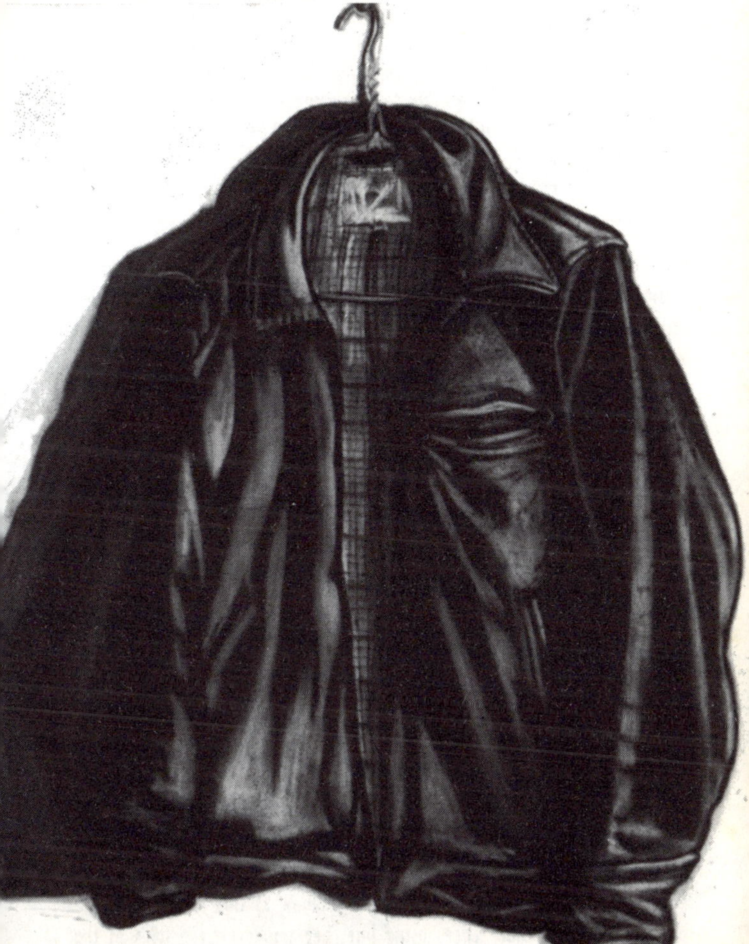

Trompe l'oeil jacket

USING EXTRA-LARGE DRAWING PAPER

If your garment needs to be drawn on a sheet of paper bigger than A1, you may be able to buy a very large sheet of drawing paper (A0 or bigger); if not, you can join two or more A1 sheets together. When you do this, butt the sides of the two sheets together without any gap or overlap, and stick a strip of masking tape along the join. The side with masking tape will be the back of the drawing.

plain colour) and that there is no patterned wallpaper. It will not help the illusion if your garment hangs too flat against the wall as there will be little contrast in tone between one part and another, so make sure that it hangs in a way that creates folds.

Your next consideration is lighting. You need to side-light the drapery with a strong light to create a strong shadow on the wall to one side. A spotlight or an anglepoise lamp with a powerful bulb work well.

The size of the garment will determine how large your paper is and therefore whether you can use an easel and drawing board. Your paper must be a little bigger than your garment so that you can draw it approximately life size together with the shadow that is cast on the wall. If your drawing paper is too large to use with your board, attach the paper to the wall next to your subject. Otherwise, set up your easel and drawing board as for previous projects.

Position yourself directly in front of the subject, so that you see it like a bas relief, and begin to draw. At first, concentrate on the overall composition, drawing the outline of the garment. Remember that the scale you are using is approximately life size; and don't forget to include the hanger and the nail or hook that your drapery item is hanging from, and any shadow that is created by them. Make the drawing fill the paper but do not touch the edges, and draw the cast shadow as this is an integral part of creating the illusion. Then, using line, begin to draw the folds of the material. This will give you a basic appreciation of how the form falls and will help you understand the fluting of the folds. The next step is to model the form using tone and texture.

Tone

The aim of this project is to do a tonal drawing using observation as a starting point, but developing the drawing by using what you know to be there. In 'Space and Light', when using chiaroscuro, you observed light and shade on objects and focused on drawing these areas of tone rather than trying to draw the object; in other words, you allowed the object to evolve through the drawing of tone. This is how you should approach an initial understanding of the form of the garment. Draw the tonal areas that fall across the drapery and the shadows that it casts on the wall.

The second stage is analytical rather than observational. Stand back and assess what you have achieved with the first process, and what is lacking that prevents the illusion from working. The next step is to develop a visual language for showing form. This is much simpler than it sounds because you will use the same method – modelling with tone – as in 'Fundamental Form'. Don't continue to draw the tones exactly as you see them; instead, try to use a system of tonal modulations to express form and space. For example, when describing a fold in the material, make the nearest point light and gradually darken the tone as the cloth recedes away from you. If part of the set-up is in dark shadow – so dark that you cannot see any detail – observe that area more closely and draw what you know to be there, not just what you see.

Texture

Finally, think about the texture of the garment and how this can be implied. This not only gives a sense of what the garment is made of, but will also help in the final modelling of the form. When the drawing is finished, if you take down the garment and put up your drawing in the same place, your trompe l'oeil illusion should be reasonably convincing.

PROJECT 2

DRAPED FORM

One 5-hour drawing

Materials: *a large object or piece of furniture, 1-2 large, plain-coloured sheets, spotlight or anglepoise lamp, window-mount, A0 or A1 paper, pencils or graphite sticks if using A1 paper, charcoal or compressed charcoal if using A0 paper, plastic eraser*

The aim of the project is to describe the forms that occur in material draped over an object, using tonal modelling.

Choose an object and cover it with the sheet or sheets. The object should have obvious form so that you can get an understanding of what is underneath the sheet, but it should have enough interest not to make a boring composition (not something as simple as a table). You could use a chair with a back and arms to it. When you have chosen the object, place it 1.5-2m (2-3 ft) in front of a plain wall. You will be using the line between the floor and the wall as a horizon line (see 'Space and Light', Project 1). Drape the sheets loosely over the object, making sure that they reach down to the floor. There should be some indication of the form of the object underneath the covering, without too much detail. Light the draped object from the front.

For this project, it is best to work on A0 (double A1) paper if you have the space. If you are working on A0 paper and you do not have a large enough drawing board to take it, attach the paper directly to the wall.

Select your composition using a window-mount. The draped object should be drawn in its environment – including the floor, walls and so on – as this will help your understanding of space. First, draw the composition using the horizon line and negative space (see 'Space and Light', Project 1). Then, observing the draped form carefully, try to describe the folds of the cloth by drawing with line.

Right: Draped form

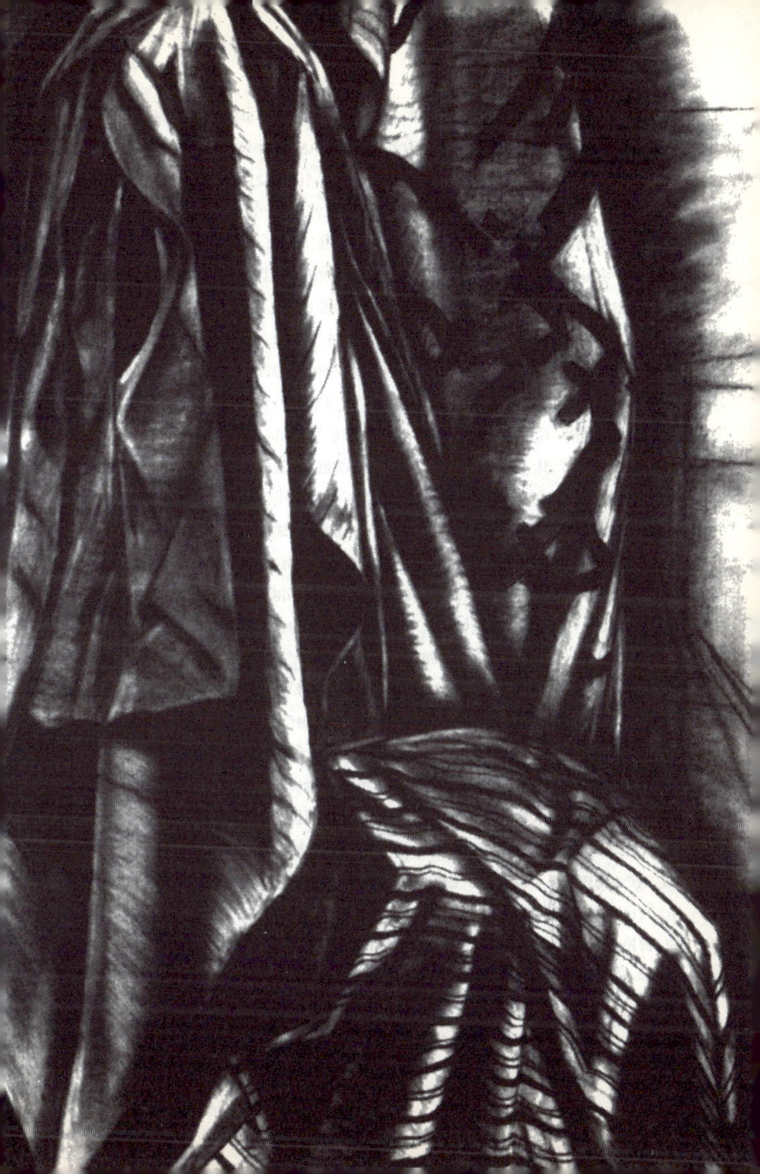

The next stage is to describe the tones in the subject. You will notice that when the form is lit from the front, the draped object appears somewhat monumental. This is because the surfaces facing you and those on top of the subject are lighter, while surfaces receding away from you get darker (unlike side-lighting, where one side is lit and the other is in shadow, and cast shadows fall from one side to the other). You need to demonstrate this tonally to create the illusion of form. Bear in mind, however, that shadows are cast by front lighting, and that there might be some folds of drapery casting shadow or contained within shadow. Remember also that you will be using a darker tonal scale for the darker areas than the tonal scale you would use for the more brightly lit areas.

On a scrap of paper make some studies of an area where the cloth is fluted. Do one study of folds that are directly lit by the light source, and you will notice that the tonal range extends from white to black. Then make a study of an area of cloth that is in shadow. You will notice that here the full range of tone is not available, and that you have to describe the form using a lower-key, or darker, tonal range. From this you should realise that in some areas it will be necessary to use very gradual tonal transitions, and in other areas you may need to use contrasting tones to show the shadow of a fold falling on a lighter area.

Next, make small studies to start to develop a visual language or system to show the form of the cloth by using a system of tonal modulations to express form and space. For example, when drawing a fold in the material, start with the point nearest to you, facing the light, and gradually darken the tone as the cloth recedes away from you. If some areas are lost in shadow, draw what you know is there, not just what you see.

When you understand this from your studies, start drawing the tonal areas of your main drawing. You don't need to refer very much to the actual draped object in front of you. You should end up with a strong, monumental drawing, showing the weight of fundamental forms, as in an El Greco painting.

PROJECT 3

WRAPPED FORM

One 5-hour drawing

Materials: *a large, tall object or piece of furniture, 2 or more large, plain-coloured sheets, window-mount, A0 or A1 drawing paper, pencils or graphite sticks if using A1 paper, charcoal or compressed charcoal if using A0 paper, plastic eraser, spotlight or anglepoise lamp*

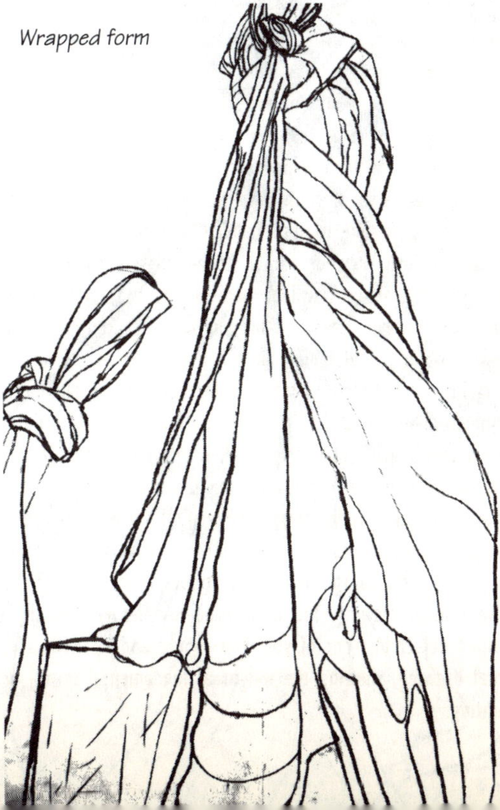

Wrapped form

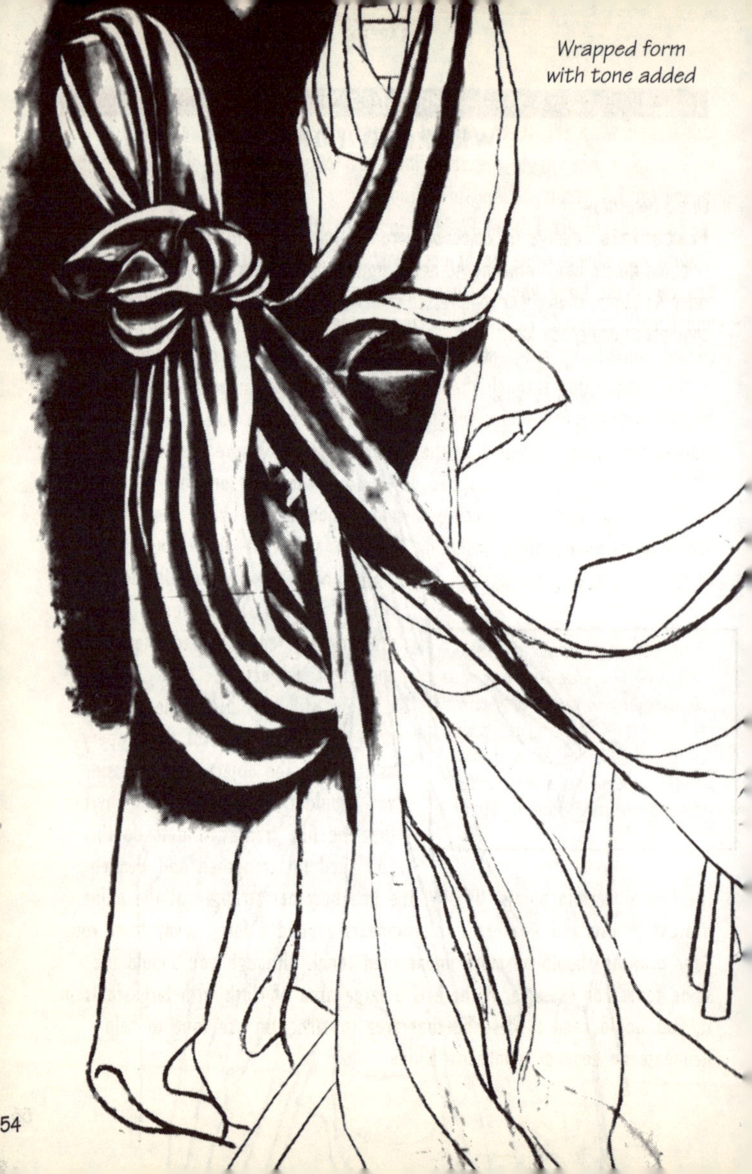

Wrapped form with tone added

For this drawing use a tall, standing form such as a coat-stand or step-ladder and wrap the sheets around it. Or you could use an easel if you have a spare one. Angle the easel forwards to give a sense of direction and movement (as occurs in Poussin's drapery).

Place the object 1.5-2m (2-3 ft) in front of a plain wall. Instead of draping the sheets over the object, twist and wrap or tie them around it. You can make large knots with a sheet, and also leave areas of the object underneath exposed. Tie and twist the sheets around the object with a closely bunched-up effect in order to give a sense of movement and tension to the composition through the way the drapes are manipulated. The twisted and wrapped sheets will follow the form of the object underneath more closely than happened in the previous project, where the sheet was loosely draped. Light the wrapped object from the front or side.

Select your composition using a window-mount. The object should be drawn in its environment, including the floor and walls. Draw your selected composition, taking the horizon line – the line between the wall and the floor – as your starting point and drawing the negative space (see 'Space and Light' Project 1).

The drawing should demonstrate the illusion of the drapery moving around the form of the object with the emphasis on line, but don't neglect tone as a device to aid form and movement.

Now, still only using line, begin to draw the linear effect of the drapery as it wraps the object. Like Poussin, you should try to establish the rhythm that the line creates, and to do this you need to strengthen and weaken the line at certain points. Usually, the line becomes stronger at the point nearest to you and weaker as it disappears around a form, away from you. Your drawing should be more linear than tonal, although you should use some tone. For example, if there is a large area of cloth with large folds in it, you would need to describe that area tonally. Also use tone to help delineate an edge or emphasise a line.

CHAPTER 5

OBJECTS IN SPACE

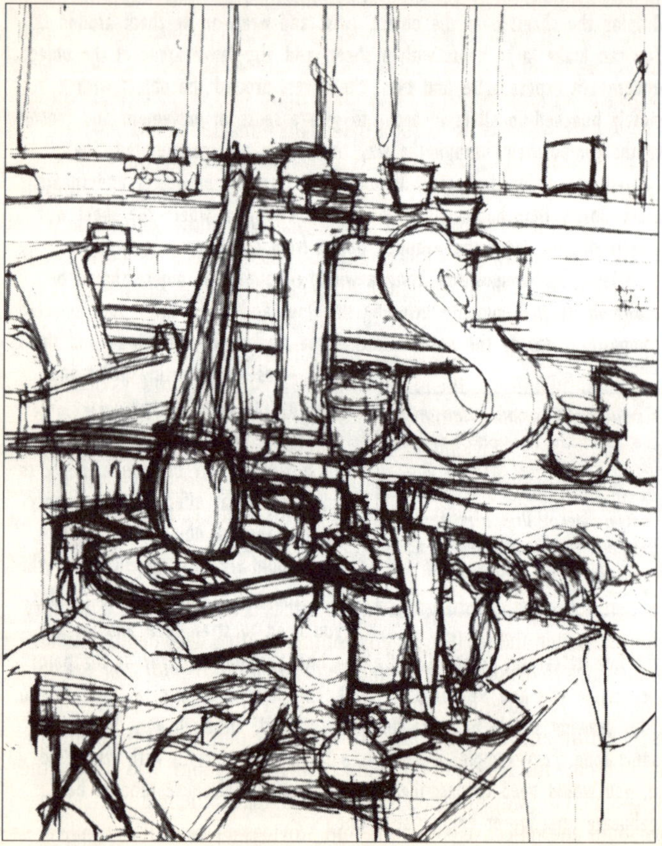

Previous projects have concentrated on the illusion of space on the picture plane, but with a relatively shallow depth of field. In the drawings in this chapter, you will be creating the illusion of a deeper space. To show this greater depth, Projects 1 and 2 involve setting up a still-life group in a room and placing the objects at different distances away from your position within the foreground, middle ground and background. The drawing will then focus on the idea of space.

Artists working with still life as their main subject have usually used a very shallow space, or depth of field. This puts greater emphasis on the chosen still-life objects, in turn allowing ideas about the subject matter to come across more clearly. In anecdotal, historical or religious pictures, on the other hand, still-life objects are usually set in a deep space or depth of field. In these paintings, the objects are subordinate to the primary purpose or content of the picture; and they often appear scattered about the scene, although they were usually strategically placed to enhance the space and composition and add symbolic or anecdotal meaning to the pictures. There are many examples of this use of still life. The Spanish painter Diego Velasquez (1599-1660) loved to use ordinary everyday objects as his subject matter and to depict them in a very naturalistic manner. For his work to be accepted, however, he usually had to place them within a religious context. His handling of still-life subject matter, nevertheless, shows that his interest lay in the portrayal of the ordinary.

Before the 20th century, only a few artists used still life as a primary subject matter and set it in an environment with a deep depth of field. Van Gogh's *Bedroom at Arles* and *The Yellow Chair with Pipe* are good examples. The latter painting doesn't have a great depth of field, but it is set within an encircling space. However, the painting of his bedroom includes the full length of the sparsely furnished room. The objects, the setting and the way in which the artist has treated them creates a very personal and reflective comment, and provides a powerful example of how objects and their environment can be manipulated to make a very poignant statement. J.W.M. Turner (1775-1851) in his interiors of Petworth used atmosphere to create a sense of space, although it is arguable whether these are studies of still life or interiors. It was only with the arrival of the 20th century that the idea of space and the understanding of objects in space were looked at in a different light.

One of the new ways of understanding the potential of objects is found in the ideas that came out of Surrealism, a movement that included artists such as Max Ernst, René Magritte (1898-1967) and Salvador Dali (1904-89), and the paintings and drawings of the Metaphysical artists, an Italian movement that included Giorgio de Chirico (1888-1978)and Carlo Carra (1881-1966). These two groups of artists began to use objects in a new context, juxtaposing them in ways in which they would not normally be observed, and placing them within a deep space, such as a landscape or a twisted interior. Their pictures evoked a type of dream world.

Although the following projects make use of spatial compositional ideas (organising the objects in a receding space), you should also try to make the still life the major focus. You should aim to render and connect objects in a relatively deep space, and each project provides a different approach.

PROJECT 1
CONTINUOUS-LINE DRAWING

One 3-4 hour drawing

Materials: *still-life objects, plain-coloured sheets, window-mount, A1 cartridge paper, 3B and 4B pencils, plastic eraser, pencil sharpener*

The aim of this project is to make a gestural drawing with a greater depth of field than in previous projects. Look at the gestural drawings of interiors by Alberto Giacometti (1901-66) as examples.

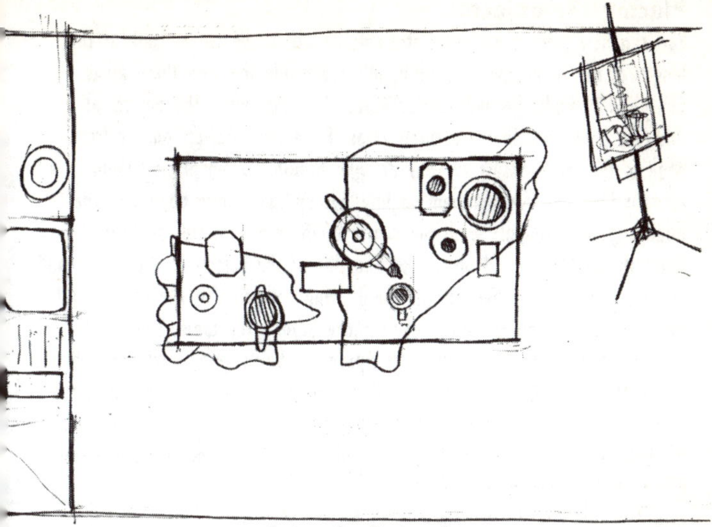

Set-up for Project 1

The best place to do this project is in a long room. Set up a table in the middle of the room; at the far end you will need something like shelves, a desk or a set of drawers – something that is slightly higher than the table – on which you can put objects. Set up your drawing board at the opposite end of the room to the desk or shelves.

Arrange the drapery over the table so that it creates links back through space. It should be arranged so that it lies along the length of the table, going away from your drawing position, rather than lying across the table. Then, when you draw the drapery, it will travel into the picture space rather than across it. The drapery doesn't have to cover the table-top completely. Arrange it so that part hangs over the front edge of the table. The drapery then acts as a visual device in the drawing by leading the eye back through the picture space.

Placing the objects

You can now place the objects strategically within the space. Look at the length of the room and in your mind's eye divide this into three areas – foreground, middle ground and background – and group the objects at different points within these three areas. Place some objects on the front edge of the table closest to your drawing position; avoid placing them in a straight line, but overlap them slightly. Set up some more objects in the middle ground (roughly from the centre of the table towards the back). Place the middle-ground objects to one side of the objects in the foreground so that you can see them from your drawing position. For the background, put some objects on the piece of furniture beyond the table. You should have created a rough, asymmetrical zigzag of objects going back through space. Once the objects are in place, manipulate the drapery by ruffling it and bunching it up around some of them.

Now select your composition. You can use a window-mount, but remember that the composition should include the whole depth of the room and the far wall and ceiling, if possible. You may need to hold the mount close to your face to include all of this.

Don't worry at this stage about accurate proportions and angles (such as the side of the table, or the line where the ceiling meets the wall), as they can be corrected later. Using the continuous line, you want to get the feel of where the objects are located in the space.

Starting to draw

You are going to start with a continuous-line drawing. This means that you do not take the pencil off the paper at all until you have drawn everything in the composition. No matter how much you are tempted, do not deliberately lift your pencil off the paper, as to do so will break the momentum of the line. However, if the pencil does come off, restart the drawing at the place where you stopped.

Right: Still life set in a deep space

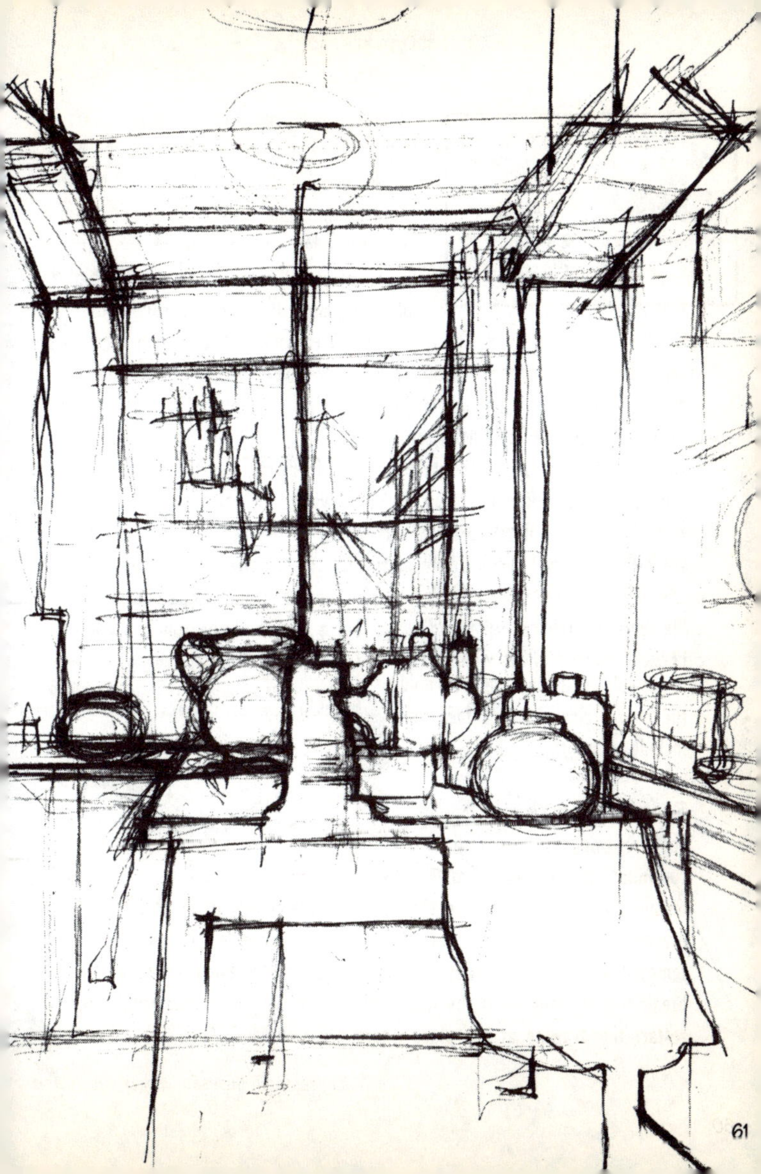

> *A line can be brought forward within the picture space by making it darker, and it can be moved back within the picture space if it is made lighter.*

Place your pencil on the paper, starting at the point where you think the edge of the nearest object is. This could be the edge of the table or a drape that hangs over the edge. Use this line as the entry point into your drawing. You could think of your pencil as a fly in a room that leaves a line behind it as it flies from one object to another and back again. The line should move back and then forwards in space, picking up sides, edges, tops and bottoms of objects, but without drawing a complete object.

Your final drawing may contain completed objects, but these will have been achieved at different stages. In other words, do not arrive at one object, draw it completely and then move on to the next object, draw that, move on and so on. The purpose of the line is to activate an understanding of the whole space. Allow the line to pick up the negative space as it moves through the drawing, and let it find a corner of the room, windows, cupboards and so on as well as the objects.

Linking objects at different points back in space

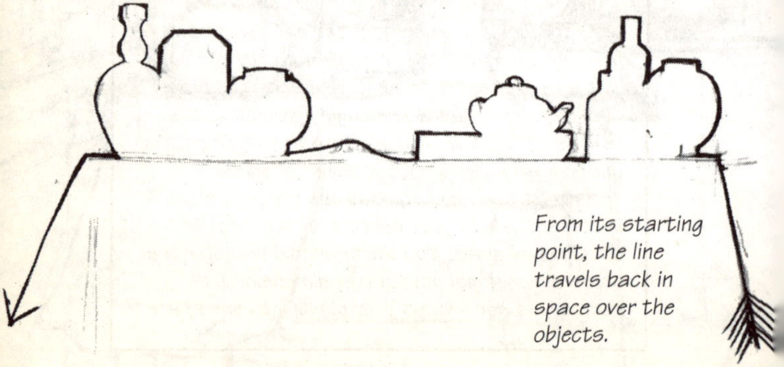

From its starting point, the line travels back in space over the objects.

The line you are drawing with is a free line – it is a line of discovery. Spend about half an hour on this stage. You should end up with a very scrawly drawing. Now you can correct and establish with line, where necessary, the perspectival angles of tables, cupboards, drapery and so on.

The next stage is to consolidate the links in space between the objects and to emphasise them. The line you are going to use now is very like the horizon line used in the early projects of the book (see 'Space and Light'), but instead of moving across the picture plane it travels back into the picture space (see diagram opposite).

With this rotated horizon line, pick up the nearest object and follow it, travelling over and linking objects, back into the space. These links should suggest themselves to you as you work. Do several of these rotated horizon lines, emphasising the objects and the depth of field. Continue to develop the drawing by putting lines in, taking them out, and putting others back in, until you feel you have expressed fully the idea of the objects in space.

ASSESSING ANGLES

A quick way to assess an angle is by holding up your pencil either horizontal or vertical to the edge of an object, such as a table, receding away from you, and judging the angle made by the edge. Is it less or greater than 45 degrees? You may find it easier to judge the angle if you move the pencil so that it is lying at the same angle as the one you are assessing. For either of these techniques you need to shut one eye and, most importantly, hold your pencil as if it is on a vertical sheet of glass. You are trying to transfer the three-dimensional onto a two-dimensional surface, so don't twist your pencil into the space.

PROJECT 2

TONE AND ATMOSPHERE – A REDUCTION TONE DRAWING

One 5-hour drawing

Materials: *still-life objects, several plain-coloured sheets or drapes, spotlight or anglepoise lamp, A1 cartridge paper, charcoal, plastic eraser*

The aim of this drawing is to show an atmospheric depth within the picture plane by using line and tone.

Use the same set-up as in the previous project or arrange a similar one. Light the set-up by directing a strong light towards the group from the front or from one side and turn off any other lights in the room to create a dramatic atmosphere. Cover your paper all over with charcoal. The surface should be completely black with no areas of white peeping through, so apply the charcoal very heavily. The technique is known as a reductive tone drawing because you take away tone rather than add it. This will help you to understand the way a direct light performs with still life and to separate the concepts of object and light in drawing.

Choose your composition through a window-mount, making sure that you include some of the foreground, middle ground, background, ceiling and walls.

To begin, use the eraser to draw with a continuous line, as in the previous project, exploring and discovering the objects in space (Step 1). The eraser will create a white line on the black charcoal surface, and will give you a free and open start. Things may look a little smudged and scrappy, but don't worry as the drawing will come later.

Once you have established the composition, begin to observe the light. Squint your eyes to simplify the areas of light and dark. Using the eraser, rub out all the lightest areas. Look at areas of tone rather than objects,

Right: Tone and atmosphere, Step 1

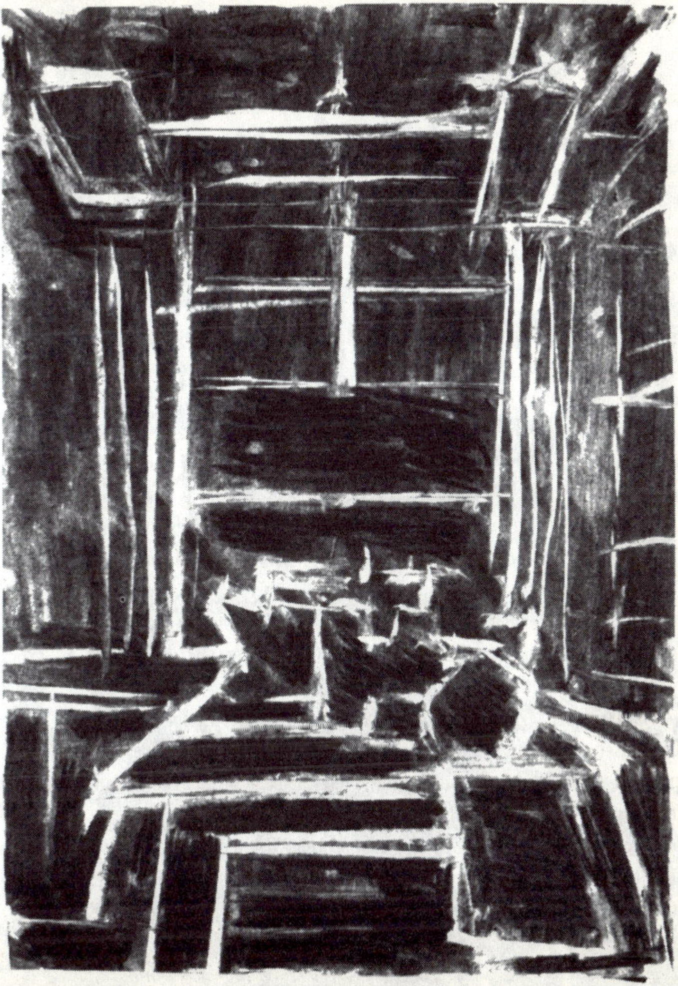

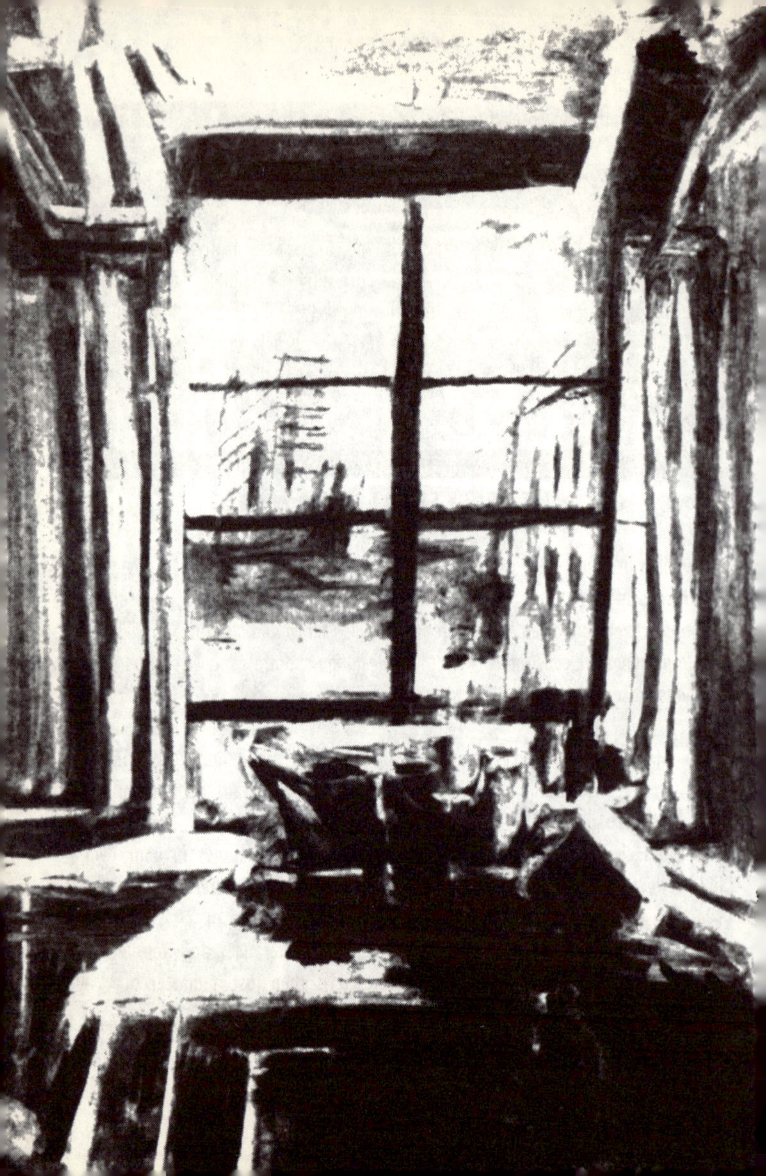

which means that in some places objects and background may fuse together as one shape.

At this point you should have a white and greyish drawing. The next step is to re-establish the black areas. Keep your eyes squinted as this will eliminate detail. You can keep repeating this process by bringing back the light through rubbing out and putting in the dark by applying the charcoal. In Turner's interiors of Petworth there is hardly any definition; light and atmosphere alone describe a deep interior space. Work your drawing until you have achieved this sense of atmospheric space (Step 2).

PROJECT 3
METAPHYSICAL DRAWING

One 5-hour drawing

Materials: *A1 drawing paper, sketchbook, pencils or graphite sticks, eraser*
Before starting this project, look at the work of De Chirico and also the Surrealists, whose paintings are constructed from the imagination and are symbolic of a personal time and place or event.

Think of objects and places that have some special meaning for you, in either your conscious or subconscious. It could be a distant memory of a place, or perhaps an insignificant object that often enters your thoughts. Or you could choose objects that reflect different times or stages in your own life. Collect these ideas, which you will use as notes and references from which to construct the drawing, by making small sketches in a sketchbook. When you have gathered a number of ideas and references and you feel your research for this drawing is complete, it is then just a matter of putting the drawing together.

Left: Tone and atmosphere, Step 2

First, consider the environment in which you are going to place your chosen objects. It needs to be an implied deep space, but it could be imagined or observed. Again, look at De Chirico and the Surrealists for inspiration. Draw this environment using line. Then place your objects in this space so that they occupy their position convincingly in the illusion you are creating. The space does not have to be in proportion or in perspective; it can be entirely imagined. Strange things might occur with the scale, but this is all right as the objects will be read symbolically. For example, you might have a giant pair of scissors leaning against a wall in the background, and in the foreground a very small peach. These two objects juxtaposed in an alien context could create the idea of threat. Draw the objects using line as you did the surrounding environment.

For the final stage, adopt a constructed method of working using tone (see 'Fundamental Form', Project 1) and implied texture. You can use an implied directional light source, which will add the idea of how shadows can become an important part of the reading of a picture. Or you can construct each individual element in the picture using tone to model the form without cast shadows. Remember that implied texture can play an important part in the meaning and reading of this drawing.

If you have enjoyed this way of working, try juxtaposing different objects in different environments. After a time, you will find that you are using objects and placing them in environments that are very particular to your personal memories, dreams and feelings, evoked by the subconscious. You will begin to create a visual resonance that is not only particular to you, but which also holds meanings of other sorts for the viewer.

CHAPTER 6

THE MOVING VIEW

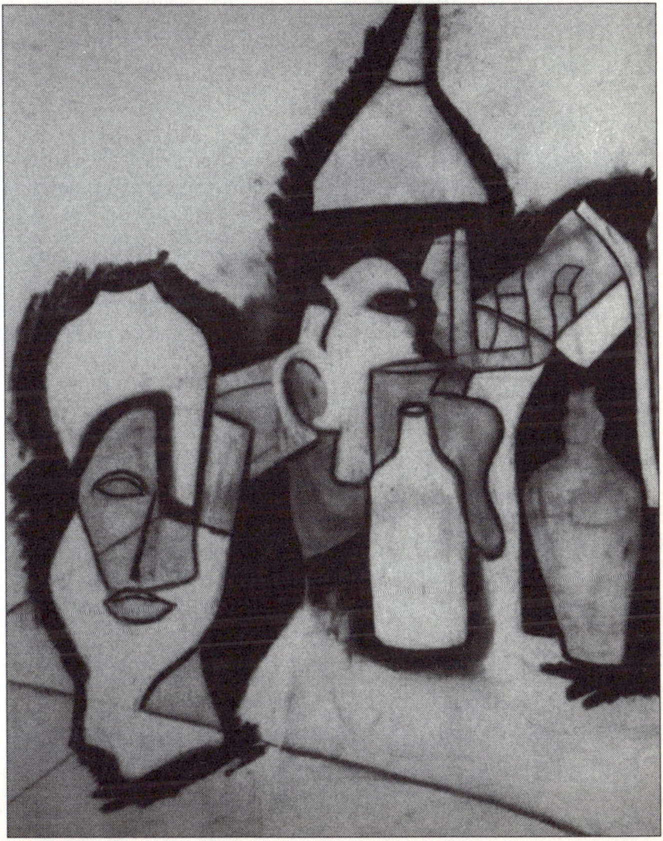

Before the beginning of the 20th century, artists depicted their subject matter from one viewpoint. Whether the subject was taken from nature or was a contrived historical or religious scene, the viewer was given a fixed position from which to read the event. It was not until the advent of Cubism at the beginning of the 20th century that artists began to question the static view of the world that had previously been presented in drawing and painting. After all, we move and objects can be moved, so why should we always work from and present a fixed position?

Before embarking on the projects in this chapter, look at the early Cubist works of Pablo Picasso and Georges Braque (1882-1963), two artists who tried to understand and present the world from a number of different viewpoints within one picture. For example, a Cubist painting of a cup might show it depicted from a side view, from underneath and from above – not presenting the cup as we see it, but trying to present what we know is there.

One difficulty with this way of working lies in the need to convey the idea that an object exists in space, in context with other objects, because the illusion of form would undermine the sense of different viewpoints. To overcome this, the Cubists used a particular system of shading that created the illusion of planal recession (many different planes, usually in a shallow depth of field, making up the picture). Their system used shading on the inside of the plane in conjunction with shading on the outside of the plane in order to make the edge of a plane appear to come forward.

In the work of the Cubists, we get a sense of space almost being twisted on the picture plane as if like a fractured space. We pick up fragments of objects seen from various angles rather than one consistent view. This approach enables us to examine the world of three dimensions on a two-dimensional plane in an analytical rather than an observational way.

PROJECT 1

SUPERIMPOSED ELEVATIONS CREATING PLANAL RECESSION

One 1-hour drawing

Materials: *still-life object, A1 cartridge paper, pencils, plastic eraser*

Studies of an object from several different viewpoints are superimposed on top of each other, which will give an insight into ways of approaching the more complex drawings in Projects 2 and 3.

Choose an object that is not symmetrical; one that has a handle or spout or something similar. A plate would not be suitable, but a teapot would work well. The first stage is to draw your object from three different viewpoints, referred to as side, top and bottom elevations.

Side elevation: Look at your object from the side and draw it using line, describing the shape of the object. Don't try to describe or imply the form of the object; instead, use outline to create the silhouette.

Top: Next, look at the object from above and make a line drawing superimposed on top of the side elevation drawing. Use the same proportions as the side elevation.

Bottom: Look also at the object from the bottom, superimposing the drawing over the previous two. Again,

Superimposed elevations, Step 1

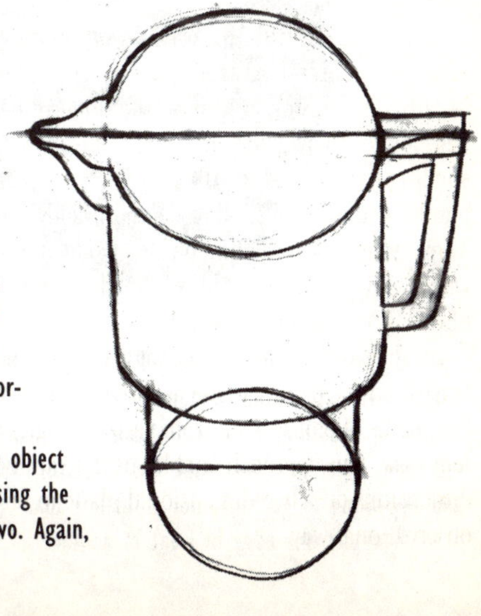

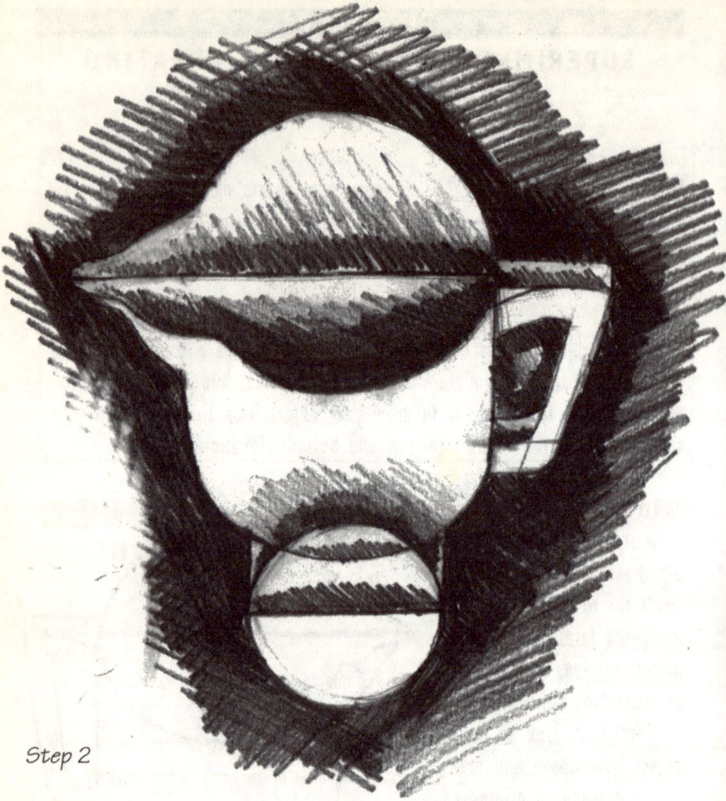

Step 2

use the same proportions. You will now have three line drawings from three different viewpoints superimposed on top of each other (Step 1).

The second stage is to add shading to create the illusion of planal recession: different planes (like flat sheets of card) overlapping each other and appearing to go back into a shallow space (Step 2). In places you will need to depict one edge in front of another.

ADVANCING AND RECEDING PLANES

To make an edge of a plane come forwards, you need to shade the area behind that edge, but you only need to shade a small area behind the front edge. This method will allow you to create and organise the spatial recession.

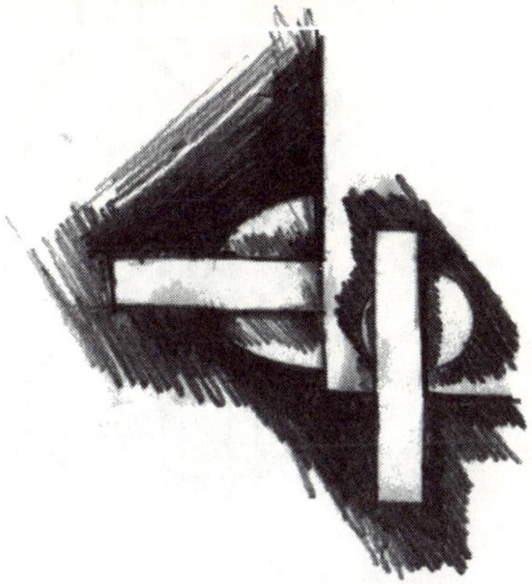

PROJECT 2

SUPERIMPOSED ELEVATIONS CREATING PLANAL RECESSION

One 4-5 hour drawing

Materials: *4-5 still-life objects (use teapots, cups, jugs, bottles, kettles etc.), A1 cartridge paper, pencils, plastic eraser*

You are going to use the same system as in the previous project, but this time include more objects. Before starting, look at some examples of the early Cubist work of Braque and Picasso.

Position a table against the wall to create an artificial horizon line and arrange the objects on it (see 'Space and Light', Project 1). Then begin to draw in line, using the negative space, and complete the objects using line only. This will help you establish the composition and the relationship between the objects.

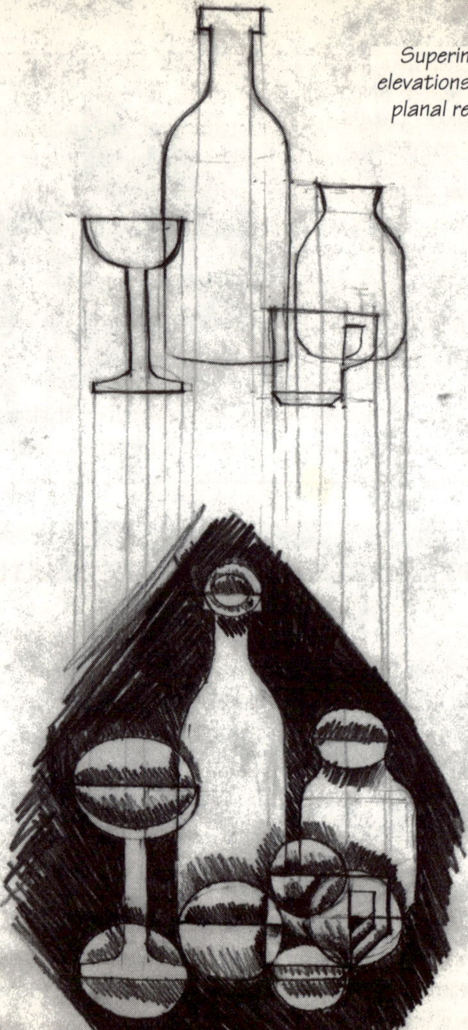

Superimposed elevations creating planal recession

The next step is to analyse each object from different elevations, as in the previous project. In the drawing you have just done, you will probably have drawn different objects in different elevations. For example, you might have drawn the front elevation of a teapot and the side elevation of a jug. What you must do now is to render each object in all three elevations, top, side and bottom, even though they might need to be superimposed over each other.

Once you have drawn all the objects from all three positions, you can begin to simplify the composition in an abstract sense. Try to balance the composition by rubbing out some parts and linking shapes and lines together. It is advisable to keep some elements of the original objects recognisable. Then add shading on the inside and outside of planes, using the same principles as in Project 1, to create a spatial illusion of overlapping and receding planes.

PROJECT 3

MOVING YOUR VIEWPOINT

One 4-5 hour drawing

Materials: *still-life objects, window-mount, A0 or A1 drawing paper, pencils if using A1 paper, charcoal if using A0 paper, plastic eraser*

The drawings in the previous two projects were based on technical observations (taken from views of the side, top and bottom of the objects). The aim of this project is to produce a drawing abstracted from three or four superimposed drawings of a still-life arrangement.

It is best to do this drawing on A0 (double A1) paper if you have a large enough drawing board. If you cannot get an A0 drawing board, use A1 paper and pencils. If you are able to use A0 paper (or two A1 sheets joined together) use charcoal.

Setting up the still life

Choose about ten objects with different forms, heights and characters; for example, jugs, bottles, vases, figurines, sink-plunger, funnel and so on. One of your objects must be symmetrical (such as a wine bottle). For this project you must be able to move all around the table on which the objects are placed. If this will be impossible, place the objects on a board (which you will rotate) on the table.

First of all, place the symmetrical object in the centre of the group. This is your anchor object: it will remain static and in the same position in all the drawings, and you will be able to take your bearings from it in the later stages if you feel completely lost. Then scatter the other objects randomly around the central object. Remember to consider the composition from each direction.

Beginning to draw

Choose your composition by holding a window-mount up to the group, and make sure that the anchor object is in the centre of the composition. Using the window-mount, start by doing a simple line drawing of the still life. Use the edge of the table as the horizon line and starting point and proceed to draw using the negative space (see 'Space and Light', Project 1). Draw the group with a simple yet sharp, clear line, with the anchor object in the centre of your drawing. Spend about 15-20 minutes on this drawing.

Second and third positions

The next stage is to draw the still-life group from the second position. If you think of your first position as 12 o'clock, the second position is at 3 o'clock. If you can't move around the table to the 3 o'clock position, carefully turn the board on which your objects are placed a full quarter, taking care not to disturb the objects. Draw the still life from this direction over the top of the first drawing, again using a clear, simple line. You should not need to draw the central object as it should still be located in the same position. You can use the window-mount again for this drawing if it is helpful to do so. Try to keep the proportions of the objects roughly the same as they were in the first drawing. This process can be daunting at first, but you must keep pushing yourself. It will become fun later.

Now repeat the process from the 6 o'clock position. The drawing will become very complex at this stage and you will probably feel agitated and confused. Don't worry about this, as out of the chaos you will create order later on. If you feel that you now have enough information you can start the final, abstraction stages of the drawing. If not, draw the set-up again from the 9 o'clock position.

Abstraction

Begin to work on the drawing without reference to the still life. This is where the fun starts, because you can control and direct the development of the drawing. You should adopt a quite free and open attitude towards creating the abstract drawing.

Spend some time looking at your drawing and think about how you need to proceed in order to create a harmonic, rhythmical, balanced drawing. Think about how lines could be linked up to make connecting rhythms and harmonies. Identify the lines that you feel are not working and take them out with an eraser, but leave the ghost of them in.

You should begin to see echoes and rhythms in the drawing – these could be lines or shapes that repeat or echo each other to create the idea of movement and space – and emphasise them.

You could play with the composition by joining shapes together and then using shading inside and outside the edges of shapes to create planal recession.

Overleaf: Moving your viewpoint

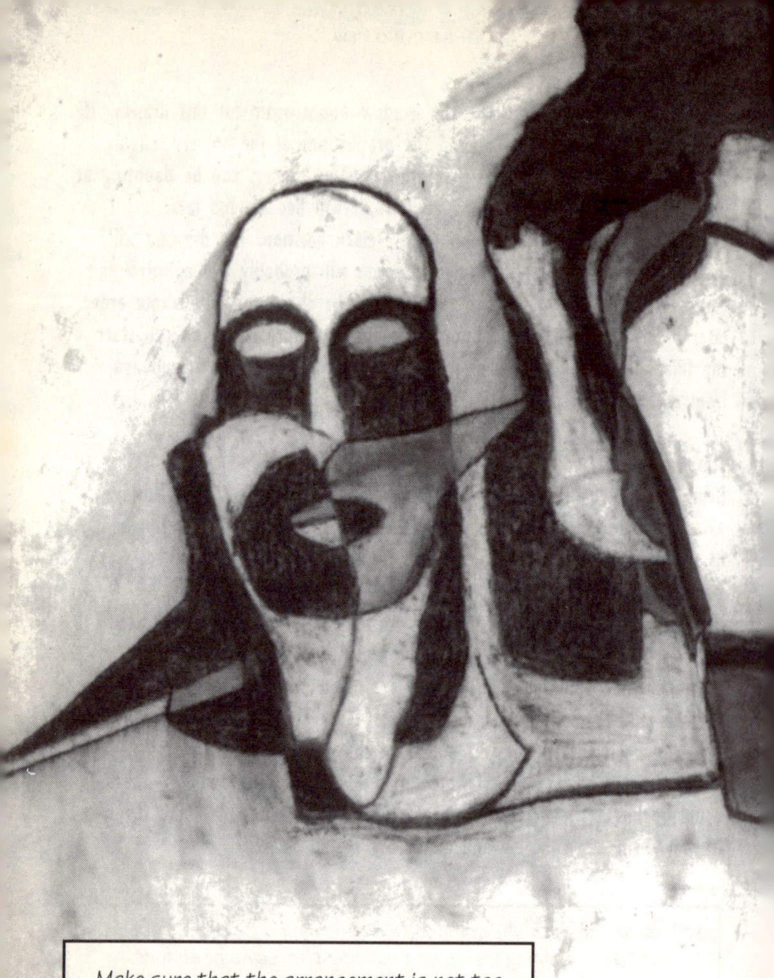

Make sure that the arrangement is not too symmetrical and that the objects are arranged at different distances from the anchor object.

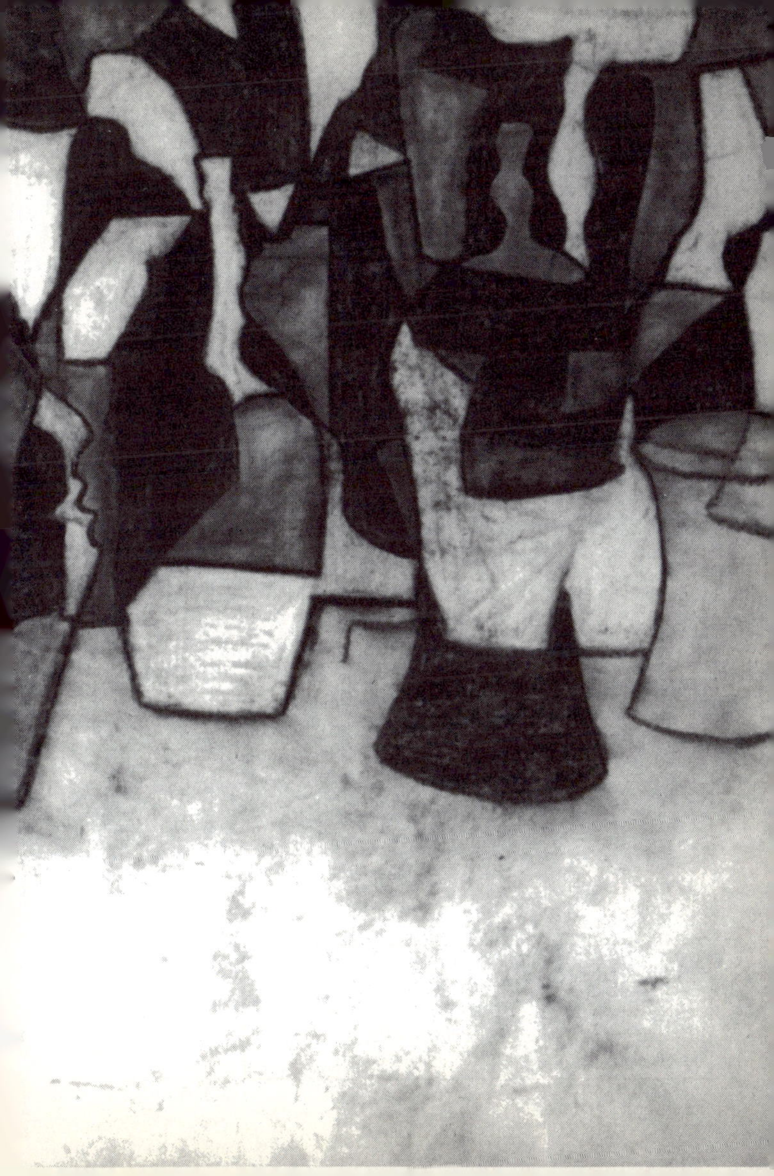

CONCLUSION

Having worked through the different drawing methods and approaches used in the projects, you should now know more about yourself as an artist and about where your strengths and interests lie. It is a mistake to think that you have to master all of these ways of working before you can progress further. Rather, you should now be asking yourself which areas and approaches were the most rewarding for you. You might have been successful with most of the projects, but which way or ways of working excited you most. And which way of working would allow you to develop your ideas further?

Once you have made these decisions, you have a whole working base to proceed from. However, do not totally put aside areas of drawing that you didn't immediately find interesting, as they will probably emerge again at a later stage in your development, and at that point you may begin to take an interest in them.

Good luck, and remember that there is no such thing as a bad drawing – it is just unfinished.

Published by Arcturus Publishing Limited
For Bookmart Limited
Registered Number 2372865
Trading as Bookmart Limited
Desford Road
Enderby
Leicester
LE9 5AD

This edition published 1996

Printed and bound in Great Britain

ISBN 1 900032 70 8

Text: Peter Stanyer

Editor: Helen Douglas-Cooper
Design: Wilson Design Associates

ACKNOWLEDGEMENTS
The authors and publishers would like to thank the following students for lending drawings for reproduction: Gaynor Baker, Paula Bodington, Francesca Cesati, Rebecca Evanson, Jane Johnson, Miriam Kelly, Sylvia Pizzinnato, Iranwin Reece, Josephine Shepherd, Janet Sum, Liz Venard; and thanks to all the students who donated drawings for possible inclusion.

The authors would like to thank the City Literary Institute and the Chelsea School of Art and Design, where they teach many of these drawing programmes.